May Your Dreams
Light the Way!

2017

On Wings
of Dreams

A Soul-Inspired Memoir

Jan Johnson

BALBOA
PRESS
A DIVISION OF HAY HOUSE

ISBN: 978-1-4525-4983-5 (sc)
ISBN: 978-1-4525-4982-8 (e)
ISBN: 978-1-4525-4981-1 (hc)

Library of Congress Control Number: 2012905699

Balboa Press books may be ordered through booksellers or by contacting:

Balboa Press
A Division of Hay House
1663 Liberty Drive
Bloomington, IN 47403
www.balboapress.com
1-(877) 407-4847

Because of the dynamic nature of the Internet, any web addresses or links contained in this book may have changed since publication and may no longer be valid. The views expressed in this work are solely those of the author and do not necessarily reflect the views of the publisher, and the publisher hereby disclaims any responsibility for them.

The author of this book does not dispense medical advice or prescribe the use of any technique as a form of treatment for physical, emotional, or medical problems without the advice of a physician, either directly or indirectly. The intent of the author is only to offer information of a general nature to help you in your quest for emotional and spiritual well-being. In the event you use any of the information in this book for yourself, which is your constitutional right, the author and the publisher assume no responsibility for your actions.

Author photographs on the front and back cover have been provided by Peter J. Crowley. peterjcrowley.com.

Printed in the United States of America

Balboa Press rev. date: 05/11/12

On Wings of Dreams *is the true account of my unfolding spiritual journey. The names and identities of all but two people mentioned, Robert Moss and Peter J. Crowley, have been changed to protect privacy. Letters from Uncle Martin are slight revisions of actual documents. Each dream is a modified version of an entry in one of my many dream journals.*

Dedication

To my parents, in loving memory, for your strong, unified intention: to create and maintain peace in our home. Separately, you taught me to dance my own dance and sing my own song. Together, you taught me the importance of holding the family close and giving from the heart. Unknowingly, you invited me to question why things happen as they do, and I am extremely grateful.

CHAPTER 1

The Bird Shooting Game

In the cool shadows of a city, I'm pushing my way into a crowd of spectators. A game is about to begin and I am taking my place up front. Thunderous cheering heightens our excitement as a virile man struts to the center of our circle and raises a polished rifle for all to see.

"He gets one shot," a voice whispers, as a caged bird is rolled in.

Silence takes over.

The marksman shoulders his weapon, taking aim a few inches above the door of the cage. Carefully, he calculates where to rest the point of his rifle; I realize, as he holds steady, he's aiming at me.

Collapsing into suddenly cold hands that press against my chest, I can barely utter, "No." My legs have folded under me, into a backward shuffling, but the tightly interlocked group resists. There is nowhere to hide.

The bird is set free. The shot is fired. The feathered body falls at my feet. Amid deafening applause, the tiny sparrow tries to right itself. I'm amazed it's still alive.

No one seems to notice the struggling, or the woman who has stepped forward. She lightly touches her hand to a trembling wing, and I ask her, "Do they put these wounded birds to sleep, let them die, or try to heal them?"

I WAS THIRTY-EIGHT WHEN I awoke from this dream. It haunted me. I knew I was the bird, and the injury had been unavoidable.

1

Wounding doesn't always happen in extreme or obvious ways, but it does happen to all of us. In the most "perfect" families, words and actions – whether intentional or not – can inflict suffering. Feelings form beliefs. What we believe to be true becomes our reality.

"The Bird Shooting Game" offered up the blueprint of a spiritual opportunity. My ambitious desire to heal that wounded bird, supported by intense studies of my nightly dreams, evolved into this account of my life's journey.

CHAPTER 2

Expectations And Promises

Nestled deep inside a faded, scotch-taped, corrugated box at the back of my bedroom closet is a photograph of my grandmother. Her voluptuous body sits tall on the campus lawn, in a soft print dress that conforms to every contour. In celebration of her first semester at Wellesley College, she extends an open bottle of wine toward the man who holds the camera, a law student who would eventually ask my grandmother to marry him. Her stubby fingers cover the label, keeping the wine selection a secret, but in one click of that camera's shutter, Grampa Everett recorded the playful image of my grandparents' first date.

Countless times I have unfolded and reread the assortment of yellowed letters that have, by some turn of fate, found their way into the same box. I'll admit, I've been digging. Savoring the sweetness of each piece of evidence like a fresh raw vegetable pulled from a magnificent healing garden. The most delicious narrative is my great-grandfather's first note to Nanny as she entered college, where he praises her for her academic achievement (ambitious for a woman in 1908). He writes what he wishes for his cherished daughter, that all her dreams come true.

I believe Nanny discovered, as the harsher reality of married life played out before her, that she wasn't cut out for the mothering role. Her words scream in a penned letter to Grampa Everett, when he was off on business and she was left tending to their three small children. Her passionately written page of rage, brought on by days of rain, messy diapers, and mischevious children, is the lasting testament to my grandmother's discontent. I remember her occasionally retelling the story of throwing a set of dishes out the kitchen window rather than washing them – one of her more humorous tirades. I'm sure she had expected much more from life.

"Your grandmother was a wild woman," I remember Dad saying when I had grown old enough to be told such a personal family truth. Funny, I can't think of many others he revealed. My mother's personality was quite the opposite; a cooler, more reserved constitution. I can imagine her standing in front of her bedroom mirror, twisting her tightly sculpted auburn waves into place, plucking a stray hair from her pencil-thin eyebrows as she reflected upon her parents' relentless conflicts. When she tired of the parental discord that resonated into the farthest corners of their ten-room Georgian home, my mother may have stared into her reflection, focusing intently on her burning commitment to create a path different from theirs. It could have been right there, in front of her mirror, where my mother promised herself, "When I get married, there will be no fighting." In her heart she felt sure that without this one element (the embroiled arguments) she could attain the perfect family. I'm convinced she discussed her pledge with my father before accepting his proposal and, in this vulnerable moment that falling in love had offered up, most certainly my father had agreed.

Creating beautiful weddings, moving into houses, and starting families are confirmations that our truest dreams are coming true. But all can be shattered quickly and bewilderingly. There is no word for what my mother became: a mother who lost a child. The fact that he was her first child, and a son, made it even harder to bear. She was pregnant with Kathleen when Eddy was diagnosed with leukemia. Kathleen's birth, a year before Eddy's passing, only amplified my mother's fears. When she and my father buried Eddy's three-year-old body in the far corner of the Granville cemetary, she was pregnant with me. Four months before I was born, my mother was forced to live through another heartbreaking ride.

One hand supported me in her bulging belly as she rolled down the car window that couldn't cool the sweltering heat. She walked into the hospital room and leaned over Grampa Everett's closed eyes, steadying us on the metal bed frame.

When her father died, I floated in my mother's devastation. She lumbered up the front staircase and into Kathleen's room, where we stood like a wide-bellied tree in the dark forest, hearing my sister's cry, unable to lift her into our branches.

CHAPTER 3
Mothers And Daughters

A wooden trunk remains open in our attic, its domed top permanently flung back on the hinges, hiding its intricate hand-carved detail, to make room for the ruffled and sequined costumes that pour over its edges. My sisters and I are hastily removing the dirty dishes from our dining-room table, two floors below, as fountains of theatrical ideas spring from our imaginations.

Kathleen, Peg, and I are giggling as we steal moments in passing. Inside our whispering we are dreaming up an afternoon performance for our grandmother, the guest of honor.

Our mother's laughter cascades over the rambling conversations. She always becomes more lively when Nanny visits from Florida. Aromas of hot apple pie and freshly brewed coffee linger around the aunts and uncles who have extended our dining table and clearing time.

"May we be excused?" Kathleen asks.

Our mother's gentle nod releases us. My older sister and I rush into the adjacent living room, through the front hallway and up the front staircase, with Peg lagging behind. The two of us break the rules when we reach the top, racing each other around the corner and up the steep attic stairs.

"Watch your step," Kathleen calls out across the widely spaced floor beams. In her smile is a silent bragging that she made it first.

I'm ignoring her, dancing on my tiptoes along a ceiling joist on an imaginary high wire above the cheering crowd I often daydream about. My dramatic dismount lands me in the tiny alcove on the only solid strip of floor. Heavy velvet costumes we aren't allowed to touch are hanging on a broad wooden pole. Those are the "good ones" our parents have worn in community theater productions and variety shows. That was how they met.

We've been granted unlimited permission to dig through the trunk, where miscellaneous selections are tangled around each other in a sparkling effervescence. Kathleen has already chosen the white tulle dress. Only a year and a half older than me, she's much taller. She'll make the adult-sized costume believable with a yellowed crinoline, a garnet sash, a delicate lift of the hem.

"Nothing fits me!" I'm moaning on my way into the mountain of fabric. I have folded my body nearly in half to reach the heavier items on the bottom. With legs dangling and arms groping, I search the darkness until the perfect accessory finds me. My toes stretch to the floor and bring me to an upright position just in time to interrupt our baby sister's next step.

"Sit down, Peg!" I call from under my four-cornered hat. I've decided to be the Jack in a deck of cards.

Kathleen is holding up one hand, like a crossing guard, to keep Peg from placing a foot on one of the narrow beams. "We'll bring you something," she promises the tiny figure with sad eyes, who has obediently frozen in place.

Without slipping once, I prance back across imagined railroad ties and join the others in a sister train, chugging back down the two flights of stairs, arms filled. The three of us tiptoe past the dining table down the cellar stairs, gathering speed in the dark cobwebbed first room, impatiently rushing into the second. A flick of the switch illuminates the joyfully pink space where Mom has taught dance classes for more than two years.

"Ladies and Gentlemen," I finally announce to the relatives, who have taken their time getting down the stairs and seating themselves as our audience. Broad velvet sleeves drop back to reveal my uplifted hands. In an unrehearsed adjustment, I push the colossal hat back on my head so I can look into the smiling faces and finish my line: "and children of all ages."

As I bounce with excitement, my skinny knees tap against the hem of the velvet jacket, sending it swinging from front to back, like a barrel worn by the clowns in my imaginary circus. Laughter sets the ice tinkling in the viewers' drinks. Nearly falling over myself, I reach toward the back corner to invoke the entrance of our first performer.

"I present to you," my voice bellows, "Kathleen Morgan!"

Like a dandelion ready to release its seeds, my big sister floats from the storage area to the upright piano that Mom recently painted bright pink. Disappearing into the mound of white netting, Kathleen closes her dark eyes under silky bangs and reopens them in a private conversation with her audience. Her short straight hair swings freely as she turns to face her music. I feverishly run behind the unpainted sheetrock wall to the rhythmic notes of her carefully practiced solo and drop my heavy costume to the floor. Peg is handing me colorfully mismatched scarves and I'm creatively covering myself, like the odd-shaped birthday package that needs a little extra paper and wrapping time.

The long pause following Kathleen's final chord evokes a clearing of someone's throat. Her eyes drift to our corner as she delicately rearranges the netting that surrounds her. Peg is nervously shaking her head, hoping for another minute, cueing Kathleen to improvise. Amid the growing chatter Kathleen taps the pedals, locking then unlocking the one on the left that sustains the vibration before reluctantly placing her fingers back on the keys.

We have been transformed into beautiful gypsies who tap their way to the center of the room. The red and black scarf wrapped around my head flows like long, silky hair. Cinched in her favorite yellow cummerbund, Peg excitedly shuffles along in tiny Chinese clogs that fit only her, marking time on a red tambourine. Wisps of chiffon flutter around us like the wings of birds as we twirl and spin without falling. Our eyes meet in an affirming moment, and we make our way to the piano for our final song. The applause lifts us up. As we run into the strong hugs, we feel the love.

"There's nothing salvageable, Emma. Honestly, I think it can all go."

The sound of Kathleen's voice has yanked my pleasant memory back to where it originated. Her brow glistening with the pink glow of menopause, she has stepped up beside me, unaware of my temporary gaze into our past. She is lifting a few unfamiliar items from the closed trunk and I realize, for the first time, the top is actually flat. There are no carved embellishments on the handcrafted box, a practical-looking container with no promise of magic whatsoever.

When I place my hands on the lid and slowly lift it, the musty smells of deteriorating velvet and tulle invite me back. Kathleen hands me a cold plastic water bottle to rinse away the dust that has already been raised in the humid August morning.

"We're here to support each other," she reminds, rolling down the edge of a black plastic bag and setting it between us like a large basket.

We drop everything in, even the glossy red Chinese clogs with a pair of tin cymbals nailed to the underside so they will jingle with every step. With the releasing of each item that meant so much to us as children, I push away the deeper feelings that are bubbling to the surface. Unwieldy garbage bags, bouncing along each step, summon memories that won't be shared today. *How many times,* I ask myself, *have I dragged my belongings up and down these stairs?*

Years ago I removed most of the antique chairs and boxes of furnishings I had asked Kathleen to hold for me. When she married Jon and bought the homestead from our parents, her offering of "temporary storage" became my "extended accommodations." Peg, and then Gina, used this familiar attic space for their own possessions along the way, also closed up in cardboard boxes and, for various periods of time, also forgotten.

Now that my sister and her husband are talking about retiring to a smaller home, the three sisters are separately arriving for a final cleanout. Except for the few remaining items on the dining-room table, all the family heirlooms that were meant to be passed on – the silverware, furniture and jewelry – have been evenly divided.

The throwing out of unusable things and passing on of heirlooms is a normal course of action. The process itself inevitably connects us to memories, like our performance in the far room of our basement. Looking back on my life, I have considered a myriad of these snapshot moments. Some evoke precious memories. Others are more disturbing. Every family has them and every family member will recount them differently.

It seems miraculous that the homestead *has stayed in our family for three generations,* I'm remarking to myself as Kathleen and I take a break and step into the yard of our childhood in silence. I'm picturing Nanny, whose energy is still alive in me, ambling across the uncut lawn to join my mother. In my mind I see them sitting together under the weeping willow tree, in Adirondack chairs that face my mother's flower garden. I can clearly make out the elaborate details on the silver ashtray that sits in my mother's lap as she looks into her violets through the smoke that rises from it.

The familiar "clink" on the arm of Nanny's chair brings a smile to my face. From the time her first grandchild was born, she was never without her gold charm bracelet. Shiny profiles dangled from the thick links, engraved with each of our names and birth dates. The jingling of flopping heads became her trademark. In my memory large straw hats shade both women's eyes, but their past has provided me with a penetrating light.

"ARE YOU SURE YOU DON'T want to go through the final pieces of glassware?" Kathleen's voice has raised me from my thoughts again.

"No thanks, but I'll take the tray with the blue butterfly."

"It was Mom's," she says, in a tone that sounds tentative. "Do you remember it hanging in the old living room?"

"Vaguely." My voice is trailing off into another thought. "I feel a strong connection to it. The butterfly is symbolic to me."

"We're definitely putting the house on the market in the spring, Emma." Kathleen has wrapped the mirrored tray in newspaper and is laying it on the floor on the passenger side of the U-Haul. "Jon has finally agreed. I hope everyone can be here on Thanksgiving so we can celebrate one final homestead holiday."

I have a hard time imagining a year passing without a Christmas or Thanksgiving dinner, a poolside picnic or birthday, at this old Georgian home. It takes an exchange of hugs to calm my stirred emotions. When my foot hits the accelerator, the pieces of carefully piled, worn-out furniture gently rattle against each other, like soft applause. My mind still lingers on my mother.

She managed a Sears and Roebuck catalogue center, sang in a Sweet Adeline quartet, and acted in community-theater productions. When she met Dad, her presence was as bright as the butterfly on her favorite tray. My mother's spirit was passionate and strong. I wish I could remember her that way as time went on.

I CAME INTO THE WORLD as Emma Eileen Morgan, on a late November afternoon, at seven pounds, five and a half ounces, with no hair, and "five dimples," my mother insisted. Filled with hunger, I longed for her physical touch, but the floodwaters of losing Eddy refused to recede. When she tentatively cradled Kathleen and me, I somehow felt my mother's eyes watching over us, like a mother bird who had found the shell of her first egg broken open by a hungry crow. Hypervigilence shifted to periods of solitude that distracted her from us.

The dance of loss and gain my family was engaged in also pulled Nanny away. Like the retreating movement in the waltz's box step, my grandmother paused when she abruptly lost her second husband, then packed up her belongings and moved away from the cold winters. I didn't know where Florida was, but I knew she would be near Uncle Henry and Aunt Rae.

My father made his decision to move to Boston, temporarily, to study to become a funeral director, "to be a better provider for our growing family," he said. I was three years old when my mother was left alone in Granville, Massachusetts, with Kathleen and me, and something I could feel but not understand: our mother's deep despair.

CHAPTER 4

Creative Gifts

"Look at how well she stays inside the lines," my mother gushed at my perfection as I brightened up a new page in an old coloring book. Without hesitation, I reached for the black crayon and reinforced her approval by thickening every outline. Color and form called me into the world of fresh possibilities. I loved losing myself there as Dad carried on an unrelated conversation that caused uproarious laughter in a corner of the room. He had finished his studies and had come home.

On the morning of Kathleen's private piano recital, I trotted down the front stairs and turned the corner into the front room where a huge, gold-framed mirror hung on the wall, a gigantic invitation to gaze into my reflection. I did this often when no one was watching; I looked deep, behind my eyes, and smiled approvingly.

A gentle tap of my mother's hand returned my attention to the formal occasion and the straight-backed chair next to Peg, facing late Grampa Everett's baby grand piano. When Kathleen took her seat and everyone's eyes remained focused on her musical abilities, I never yearned to sit in her place. When I had taken piano lessons, I realized almost immediately that acquiring the perfect piano technique required something I was unable to grasp. Why would the notes for the right hand have different letters from the notes for the left, even though they stood on the same line or space? *Confusing,*

I thought. *This is way too hard.* Rather than perfecting the suggested pieces, I spent my practice time hidden away in the basement, at the pink piano, improvising my own notes and chords, which turned out to be my parents' reason for pulling me out of piano lessons altogether.

I returned to the basement; the magical hideaway where all cares were lost in the swirling of spontaneous, unrestrained dancing and dreaming up delicious fantasies drenched in warm spotlights. Here, I was both master of ceremonies and the wild gypsy, directing Peg or playing on my own, to vinyl records of Grieg and Chopin, until the melodies could barely be heard above the scratches.

ANTICIPATION GREW INSIDE OUR CLASPED mittens as four of us now stood together, wrapped in wool scarves, at the end of our street. Three miscarriages had preceded Gina's arrival. Three attempts at replacing the son that had been lost.

"Wait with me, Gina." My responsible voice overrode the playful one as I squeezed her tiny hand. Squealing brakes and an unexplained whoosh released from the Greyhound bus as it came to a halt, the door aligned directly with us.

Like an accordion in Lawrence Welk's orchestra, it folded back and there stood Uncle Leonard. He was actually Dad's cousin, but in a family meeting we girls had unanimously decided to call him "Uncle" when he began visiting us every weekend. He had been designated the bedroom on the second floor in the back of the house, and his bags were always packed with sweets and long-playing records of the latest Broadway musicals.

No one would say it, but I was beginning to suspect that this white-haired relative had also secretly become Santa Claus. Anticipating the extra-special seasonal surprises that he had stashed away for later, we hugged him from both sides.

Kathleen pulled the albums out of the closet. I chose the one with yellow stars framing the pictures of Bing Crosby, Doris Day, and Andy Williams. Carefully slipping the record out of its sleeve, I placed it on the turntable, gently setting the needle at the smooth outer edge. The opening notes of *Joy to the World* sent everyone scurrying.

Gina and Peg flew to the attic to drag the box of window candle lights down the steep, narrow stairs. Eager for the crèche scene to be unpacked and set out, I carefully moved Eddy's bronzed baby shoes from the front room mantel to the bookcase in the upstairs hall. Mounted on a black marble base, they stood together, toes facing front, with the laces tied in perfect bows; standing strong as a constant reminder that there had once been a fifth child.

All the way to Caldwell's Farm and back, we sang the familiar songs with occasional descants that Dad had taught us over the years. With pink cheeks and wide smiles, we dragged the perfect tree up the walk and through the front door, Kathleen leading the way to be sure the tree skirt was placed exactly right. Mom was waiting with a tray of gray melamine cups filled to the top with steaming hot cocoa.

THAT CHRISTMAS MORNING UNFOLDED LIKE all the others: the opening of our stockings and the rush into the front room where a special surprise waited for each of us under the tree. Mom was lost in the background as Dad took his place passing out the few gifts that had been carefully wrapped and set underneath the tree. He carefully chose and passed out each gift individually, to extend our opening time. We had learned to stay present, watch and respond to each uncovering as we patiently waited our turn to unwrap a gift.

"Wow," Dad exclaimed; his eyes twinkled. "This one's for me." He was shaking the little package and listening for clues. We jumped up and gathered closer as he opened the handmade card and looked back to us with a smile. "From the girls."

Carefully peeling off the scotch tape without tearing the paper, he allowed the wrapping to drop to the floor and held up our simple offering, a six-pack of cigars. "This is just what I needed." His words brightened each face in the circle of daughters. "I have only one left."

I'm sure our mother's smile met his, as we spun our web of traditions and sat in his teaching of how to receive all gifts.

CHAPTER 5

Journey Of Change

Why I was the child chosen to join my grandmother in a travel adventure remains a mystery. My sisters can't recall much of the summer I went missing, one month before my fourth-grade school year recessed. This season of transition was barely noticeable to those who stayed home.

Clutching the handle of my straw basket pocketbook with one hand, I released the other from my father's grip, extending it to the waiting stewardess who walked me all the way to the tail of the plane. "The safest place to sit," my mother had said. I slid back into my reserved seat holding my arms high so the tall, uniformed woman could buckle me in.

Bright sunlight bouncing off of the window glass reflected back my widening eyes as the roaring engines thrust us into an almost upright position, like a rocket taking off into outer space. The rivers and roads, passing clouds and coastline seemed to guide the way. When we dropped, and dropped, toward the palm trees that magically sprouted from the ground, I couldn't help but call out to them, "This must be paradise."

It seemed to take forever for the other passengers to pull their baggage from the overhead compartments and bounce, shoulder to shoulder, toward the front of the plane, like cattle being prodded toward a small gate. My guardian extended a hand and I gripped her long fingers with all of mine as she escorted me along the same path, down the long passageway that corralled us into the airport. My hands felt numb from squeezing, ears searching for the familiar tinkling of the charm bracelet that accompanied Nanny everywhere. The jingling that always made me feel as if an angel was near must have been my very first memory of her.

Suddenly I heard it, and caught a glimpse of silvery white hair, glistening like snow. My arms flung open and I latched onto her generous girth.

SAN ANTONIO, TEXAS. CUPERTINO, CALIFORNIA. *How far are they from Florida?* I wondered as we climbed aboard a Greyhound bus heading west. Excitedly I began to count the states. Between visits with Nanny's friends and family, I contentedly sat in the reclining seats of the string of buses. As we soared through unknown territory, I absorbed the changing colors and shapes that flew by, sensed the sunlight flickering through my closed eyelids as I curled up and fell asleep at my grandmother's side. I think we were riding through Louisiana for the second time when Nanny took hold of my wrist and stared at my palm with the concentration of a fortuneteller.

"You have aristocratic hands, you know." She was pointing out why my fingers were long and thin. I didn't dare tell her I was ashamed of my hands. Translucent skin and protruding veins made them seem old, almost ancient looking, but I sweetly nodded at her proud discovery. Having ancestors who came across on the *Mayflower*, she pointed out, was something to be proud of. Secretly, I would rather that she called me by a special nickname like the one she called Kathleen. I had not yet learned that "Little Indian Eyes" was not an endearing term, but a derogatory slip of the tongue to let my father know she suspected a most embarrassing Native American link in his ancestral chain.

During my three-month excursion as an "only child," the goings-on in Granville had fallen away like the whisper of a dream. When we crossed the fourteenth border, on our return to Florida, my grandmother gave me the ultimate compliment: "You're a good little traveler, Emma."

DARKNESS EVENTUALLY CARRIED ME HOME, along the familiar roads and through the front door. My excitement had drifted as I fell asleep in the car. I was re-acclimating in the dim light of our front hall when Dad dashed past my mother and me, trudged up the front stairs with my single piece of luggage, and dropped it on the landing. I glanced curiously to the left and then straight ahead, my eyes resting on the doorways that had always been open. Tonight, both doors were closed.

"It's late, Emma." My mother pressed her hand gently against my back, guiding me toward the stairs. With every step, my straw basket pocketbook dropped lower to the ground and I paused at the top of the staircase. Looking through the eyes of the "good little traveler," I peered through the shadowed hallway, into the spare bedroom, and was convinced I saw furniture from the first-floor living room.

"You can see it in the morning," my mother said, encouraging me forward, through the next doorway. The bed that Uncle Leonard slept in when he visited had been moved out of the back bedroom and sat awkwardly near the foot of the attic staircase.

"Try not to wake your sisters," she said, kissing my forehead and sending me up the first few stairs. I quietly climbed to the third floor where our partially finished bedrooms had been moved before I left. Thankfully, here, my absence hadn't brought about any change.

IN THE EARLIEST LIGHT I wandered down the front stairs alone and headed straight to the gilded mirror in the front room to look at my face, to see if the change I felt inside myself was visible. The sparkle in my eyes was the same, a few new freckles. Maybe I looked more grown up.

The subtle smell that would soon become commonplace rushed into my nostrils, pulling my attention outward, to the reflection of what stood behind me. Clusters of flowers framed the dead body laid out in a casket at the opposite end of the room. Padded wooden folding chairs bordered the central aisle that lead to the old man whose bloodless face, paralyzed by death, had been touched up with color that would have been unnatural in life.

I moved closer to him, wondering if, at night in the glow of the torchiere lamps, his grotesque makeup might soften in the tearful eyes of mourners. He seemed peaceful against the gold brocade drapes that covered most of the wall behind him.

On the other side of the doorway I could see that our living room had become an office. An electric organ had replaced our baby grand piano. My curiosity nudged me to continue walking, to turn the knob that once allowed entry into our den. I stepped inside a chamber I imagined would only be found hidden in a dark cellar.

Unable to take my eyes off the long porcelain table, I let them wander along its perimeter. A wide trough ran completely around it, and a deep white tub had been installed below its gaping drain. I knew that embalming bodies was part of my father's business; preparing them, so they would last longer before they had to be buried. It had something to do with putting a preservative in their veins. I quickly slipped back into the office, carrying with me all I wanted to know about the gruesome procedure.

The walls were a comfort. The windows hadn't changed, but when I pulled aside the narrow gold drape that closed off our dining room, I could barely recall a past holiday dinner. Where the hutch and serving table had stood; silver, bronze, and mahogany caskets were now mounted against the wall, one row above the other. I slid my hand over the velvet linings that poured out of each opened box like pastel-colored whipped cream.

My mind clamped shut, locking in the feelings that my world had been swallowed up by a funeral home. *The changes have been made,* my mind told me. *We can't change them back.*

No one ever inquired about my feelings regarding the change. I could only make up my own story about what was true. Niggling impressions prodded me to believe *I must not be worth an explanation. I've been abandoned by my own family.*

My summer adventure immediately evaporated in the reality of our new existence, living over a funeral home. We had been taught what my mother had promised herself: Negative emotions will be held back and not expressed. And so it was that inaccurate beliefs would begin to grow inside me. *A good girl doesn't rock the boat.*

CHAPTER 6

Pink Paint, Blueberries, Indian Eyes

Mom brilliantly focused our attention on the attic, where our four bedrooms were still taking shape on plywood flooring within recently added half-wall partitions. We painted my room a soft pink, the color of cotton candy, and it became a personal sanctuary that stood in luminous contrast to the dark main floor of the house. Only the kitchen, with barely room for a table and six chairs, had remained intact. I hated that room. As dinner time neared, only an actively growling stomach could force me to enter.

"Eat a slice of bread if you're hungry." My mother sighed as she pulled the cigarette from her mouth. That familiar sigh registered in me as the overwhelm of feeding six on a constantly fluctuating budget. I reached into the bread box and grabbed the twisted empty part of the plastic bag.

As she scraped at the ground-meat drippings that had stuck to the bottom of the cast iron skillet, I took a seat at the table. From my mother's loosely secured french twist a few wisps of hair hung. She twirled one around her ear as she poured the can of tomato sauce over the hamburger. My fingers nervously pulled the white center out of its brown crust and rolled the dough into a perfectly round ball as I looked away, out the window, to the dimming afternoon. The Morgan Funeral Home sign stared back at me from the end of our driveway, advertising the new business that hadn't sparked much of an interest. The growing frustration my mother carried felt to me like hopelessness. I noticed it most while she was preparing meals. Any verbal complaints might stir up disharmony. She had made her passionate personal commitment never to summon them, and so we shared these awkward silences. She had chosen to keep peace at all cost, and there was no way I could keep from absorbing her unacknowledged distress.

"I saw Andrew Clayburn at the hospital today." Dad opened his conversation over dinner. "He makes the rounds to all the old sick people. He talks to their families, tells them how sorry he is." My father's monologue ran like the juices from my sliced beets into my mashed potatoes. "Andy's a crook. He's just trying to drum up business."

With my fork I drew a line of separation and pushed the burgundy portion away from the white. Poking the tines into the darker half, I quietly blended until it all turned pink. My mother sat at the opposite end of the table, allowing him to go on as I retreated into my hardening shell.

We could never tell if Dad was going to share one of those angry mealtime lessons or a joke he had just heard. Neither seemed to be considered improper to be shared with four young girls.

"...and two quarts of milk," he chuckled across the table with both hands cupped and lifted to his chest as if he were shaking two melon-sized breasts. This was his joke of the day: a woman acting out her grocery list from a window to her deaf husband on the street below. It wasn't much different from his other stories: the unique spelling class with a new student named Archibaldass Holebroke, or the nervous ticket salesman who asked if the voluptuous woman wanted her change in nipples and dimes. When our father's laughter encouraged us to join in, my confused feelings burrowed inside me, where no one would be able to interpret and judge them. As our mother let him entertain or "get things off his chest," she may have taken her personal commitment to peace one step too far.

The word "inappropriate" was never used when terms like "peckers" and "assholes" found their way into Dad's routines. After a few drinks, party guests inevitably begged him to "tell the one about..." He never failed to bring up just the right story to embellish the subject of any discussion. To me, this was a gift gone terribly wrong.

The dinner table continually gave Dad the opportunity to entertain and give his commentary on life, but it was not the place my grandmother chose to dislodge the king from his throne. When she visited, she flung her comments in from the sidelines. Pulling Kathleen to her bosom, she'd nearly suffocate her, unaware that the chain of precious gold heads was pressing against the side of my sister's face, reddening her ear.

"How's my Little Indian Eyes?" she'd ask, making sure my father was within earshot.

As the scotch took hold, Dad became immersed in his latest irritations. "Now they're calling retarded people *special*," he bellowed. My stomach tightened. "What makes retarded people *special*?"

There was never a contrary word from any of our guests, closely seated around our dining table. He would simply take control of another Thanksgiving dinner. One by one, Kathleen, Peg, Gina, and I would excuse ourselves to clear the dishes. The air felt lighter halfway down the back stairs.

At the kitchen sink, we broke into the three-part harmonies of *Dona Nobis Pacem*, a prayer our father had taught us during long trips in the car. We began every holiday dinner by singing it, and from the kitchen a pleasant round would rise again to soothe our weary guests.

"It means grant us peace," Dad had explained.

THERE WAS NO WAY I could understand my father's aggressive behavior. I simply tried to avoid him by staying in the basement or out of the house. In the early summer, Peg and I found a secret and wild bounty along the railroad tracks that led to Shatford's Pond and we scrounged around the alcove under the cellar stairs for a few aluminum containers, returning to the kitchen ready to go.

"You're going blueberry picking?" We nodded to Dad as he sat over his morning coffee. "You'd better cover yours." He was smirking as he gestured to the tiny nubs protruding from my chest. Peg giggled. "Or are they more like fried eggs?" he added.

I pushed my feelings down where they could almost be forgotten, but still lugged my father's thoughtless words with me. At the end of the day, I sat on my bed with knees tucked to my chest, arms wrapped around them. *It's just as well I don't have big breasts,* my thoughts spoke into the felt eyes of my teddy bear. *What might happen if I did?*

CHAPTER 7

Loss Of Innocence

L avender shadows widened across Kathleen's empty room. My vacant stare slid down the folds of her plain cotton curtains, across the unfinished plywood floor and back to my mirror, where my eyes rested on the reflection of the thick brown waves I was weaving into two short braids. My sister's high academic scores and our financial deficiency had secured a scholarship that allowed Northfield School For Girls to abduct her for the second year.

I guess everything became complicated that fall, when Kathleen returned to the private high school. Our birth order felt altered. The second child had become the first. The sensitive daughter became the eyes and ears of the family.

"Vicky's here," my mother called from the front hallway. My next-door neighbor and I were going to be "holding down the fort" so my parents could spend an evening with friends. Vicky held up a heavy paper bag at the bottom of the stairs and I smiled from the top. We both headed for the kitchen.

A comforting roasted smell rose from the Jiffy-Pop container that snapped and grew into a monstrous foil bubble as I shook it over the largest burner. Peg and Gina raced down the back stairs and joined in the preparations, pulling the large popcorn bowl and four tall glasses from the cupboard. The pale green Coca-Cola bottles Vicky had brought along dripped with the humidity of the early

September night. These treats would be enough to bribe my younger sisters into an early bedtime so my best friend and I wouldn't miss a moment of our annual ritual: the judging of the Miss America Pageant.

I drew three columns on the lined paper for grading the formal gown, swimsuit, and talent competitions. Stunning contestants were already parading across the stage, displaying ribbon banners that pledged allegiance to their home states. I could feel the excitement rising from my deepest desire to become just like them.

Despite my unruly hair and slowly developing breasts, I was feeling more confident when I looked down at my hands and admired my sculpted nails glistening under a fresh coat of clear polish. My mother's offer to pay me ten dollars had worked. I no longer bit them.

My pencil tapped on the white paper as I considered every imperfection. Surely I could single out the judges' choice. The decision maker for me was always the talent competition, my favorite part of the evening.

The dry piece of skin on my thumbnail had been distracting me for over an hour; that point of contrast between the glassy polish and the rough edge. When Miss California took the stage and grasped her microphone, I placed my thumb between my teeth and chewed until the commercial break. I jotted down the number eight before dashing into my parents' adjoining bedroom where the little drawer in my father's bedside table held a pair of nail clippers, right in the front. I jerked it open.

"Vicky," my voice was barely audible above the television. "Come here." A yellowed booklet had fallen forward and I was holding it in trembling hands.

"Oh my God," she gasped.

At the edge of my parents' bed we sat, rendered speechless by the naked woman folded over the arm of a couch. The man's penis that disappeared into her from behind looked as wide as a tree limb.

On our television screens Rob and Laura Petrie slept in flannel pajamas in separate beds. Until this moment, the act of sex had remained as ill defined as the rising smoke from my father's late-night cigars. Huddling together behind inarticulateness, staring into the pages where intrigue and terror merged, I felt my jaw clench at another woman's ecstatic expression with semen splashed across her face. We stared into the wordless page, then turned to the next and stared again. Another photograph, and another, and another. Within the walls of our painful initiation, our minds had shut out everything except the visual unfolding before us. In our amplified focus we sat deafened to anything else.

"Emma!" Vicky's voice startled me. She flew off the bed, disappearing into the next room. I heard them. *Are they outside or at the bottom of the stairs?* The drawer was still open. I threw the book into its hole. *Was it farther back? I'm taking too much time.* I repositioned it, slammed it shut, raced through the door, falling to the floor beside my partner-in-crime. I was grasping my notes like the rope to a life raft when my mother stepped into the room. "Who won?" she asked.

"We don't know yet," I reported back without lifting my eyes from the frenetic tallying of my scores. *We made it. She doesn't suspect a thing.*

Stunned between one reality and the other, Vicky and I waited for the final announcement. My mother left, but we didn't move until Burt Parks began to sing. A hammering applause broke loose for the crowned perfection of feminine beauty that strutted down the runway for all to admire.

With a swift "Goodnight," Vicky was gone.

"SOMETHING'S BEEN DISTURBED IN MY bedside drawer." My father's voice was calm as he dished kielbasa and noodles onto our plates at dinner the following night. He was deliberately studying us, igniting the fire in my face that burned away any attempts at acting natural. I was ambushed as my mother remained mute and he took control. By placing the blame on me, he lifted all responsibility from his own shoulders.

"I don't expect any of you to be going into places you don't belong." My father's voice stung. "Whichever one of you was responsible, you know who you are. I'm sure this won't happen again."

Why am I bad for finding something kept in a drawer we have all opened? No boundaries had been set with this one, like the unreachable drawer in his "high boy" dresser, where his rifle was kept. "Don't ever go in there," he had said. "The bullets are in a separate place. Don't ever go looking for them." He had been extremely clear.

No one had the capacity to explain to me what had fallen into my hands. Sex obviously had a dark and secret side that was to be overlooked, like Dad's nasty jokes. But more important than any confusion or anxiety over the sexual material I had come upon, I was growing to fear the practice of silence.

CHAPTER 8
The Note

When Vicky called, I made my escape alone, running across the street with my half-buttoned coat hanging off one shoulder. April-scented March air relieved the heaviness that had hung in the house since Nanny's message arrived. Illegible handwriting scrawled across a notecard revealed the extent of her recent stroke. In remarkably few words, she expressed to my mother that she would be returning to Granville. "To die," my mother had told us.

Vicky took the lead as we headed for the brook behind her house. I leaned down to touch a lustrous snowdrop, forcing my mind to push away the image of my father closing up the dining table and rolling it into a corner. A hospital bed had been carried up the front stairs. Nanny's final wishes would reclaim the lost bedroom.

In the days that followed, Peg and I focused on preparing basement accommodations for our Florida relatives who would be arriving at the end of May. Nanny seemed to wait for them. What other reason could cause her to hang on for so long? She had forgotten who we were.

My mother floated in and out of a stoic trance that I had once felt from the shadowy depths within her. Now I observed her dreamlike state in the flickering summer light, and felt the poignant, unbreakable flow of love from daughter to mother to daughter. It was a painful natural cycle: the compassionate tending to one who is nearing death. In our basement, a dehumidifier pulled the damp air in and miraculously placed it, drop by drop, into a plastic bucket below. I had the feeling that my grandmother's spirit was being released from the physical in the same way, back to the ether like the droplets of water, allowing her spirit – drop by drop – to return to the heavens.

"You kids need to stay outside until we tell you you can come in," Uncle Henry said on the afternoon Nanny died. We knew they were waiting for Dad to return home and neighbors to be assembled to help carry her body down the front stairs and into the embalming room. Eventually she was placed in a silver blue casket and laid out in the chapel. We waited for an invitation to view her.

With white hair shimmering in the gentle pink of the torchiere lamps, Nanny looked beautiful, resting comfortably like the old man who had surprised me six years before. I suddenly realized I would never again hear her laugh, her intellectual discussions sparked from articles in the *New York Times*, her jokes remembered from *Reader's Digest*. Our passionate games of Scrabble were gone forever. The reassuring jingle of Nanny's charm bracelet would be buried with her. Like the bobbing gold heads that had been dropped and replaced, her passing reminded me that life is a chain of inevitable change. We adjust and go on.

CHAPTER 9
Messages From Beyond

With graduation less than three months away, I was imagining the gateway to freedom from the pressures I had carried for the past four years. I hadn't followed in Kathleen's steps by packing up and trudging off to Northfield, but it wasn't because the opportunity hadn't been offered. In failing the entrance exam, I had disappointed myself in disappointing my parents – who never spoke a word of it. I had grown tired of trying to explain why my grades didn't get better, why the college courses didn't seem to fit. Art and gym classes provided the relief to keep me going. I hadn't applied to any colleges, and my parents hadn't forced me to. At this point, whatever the future held, I was ready to get on with it.

After a Sunday night Youth Fellowship meeting, my friend Howard offered to drive me home. From behind the wheel he noncholantly leaned toward me and made an announcement. "I have someone I'd like you to meet, Emma," he said. "A spiritual friend," he specified, lifting his eyebrows above his wire-rimmed glasses, awaiting my response. Howard was kind and responsible. He sat in the front of every class, and I couldn't understand how he could enjoy studying so much. I guess hearing him say the word *spiritual* had peaked my interest. "If you're interested," he thoughtfully added, "maybe we could go to see her next Saturday."

THE ELDERLY WOMAN LEANED FORWARD, draped in a hand-crocheted shawl, beckoning us into her den.

Howard placed his hand at my waist, encouraging me to step closer. "Emma, this is Helen." The scent of spices drew my immediate attention to the bowl of clove-studded oranges on the woman's mantel. The musty smell reminded me of Vicky's house, when her grandmother was confined to a wheelchair and windows were rarely opened.

"Hello," I nodded, before Howard's fleeting introduction detoured into a personal conversation, allowing me to contiue my visual wandering about the room. A prismed lamp illuminated a bible on the table at Helen's right hand. Maroon brocade curtains hung over a needlepoint stool that had been tucked alongside a spindly desk. To the sounds of a fading discourse, my private investigation opened up the possibility that I had seen a desk like this somewhere before, maybe in Vicky's old barn, near the spinning wheel. Howard's voice startled me.

"Oh, I'm sorry. What did you say?"

"Helen has a message for you," he repeated.

A message? I stared into his glasses without replying. To relieve my rising discomfort, I clutched the arms of the sturdy little chair, lifting it to shift my position more to the right so I could fully face the old woman. Her eyes squinted, closed, then slightly reopened.

"You're sitting in a rocking chair," she said.

I looked down to confirm. *I'm not sitting in a rocking chair.*

"I see you holding a baby in your arms. He's your brother."

My brother?

"You have a brother?" Helen inquired.

"I had a brother," I heard myself say. "He died at three and a half, before I was born."

"You're holding your brother and you're turning the pages of a book."

I brushed my hand over the tiny hairs that had raised on my forearm. "I'm reading to him?"

"You're turning the pages of a book," she repeated.

A kind of mental fog rolled in, blurring most of the information that followed. I couldn't let go of her knowing about Eddy. Howard didn't even know about him. How had *she* come up with such a precise and personal statement? What did it mean?

When we thanked Helen for seeing us, Howard casually reached into his pocket and pulled out a few pre-folded bills and placed them in a small box marked "Donations." Our quickening footsteps on the cement walk were the only sounds until I seized the car door handle like it was the wheel of a careening ship.

"Who is this woman?" I squawked across the roof of the car.

"She's not just a friend, Emma." Howard disappeared inside. I slid into the passenger seat to hear the rest. "She's also a medium at the Spiritualist Church. I attend their services every Sunday. Channeling is an integral part."

"A Spiritualist Church?" I thought he was a Methodist.

"Yes, I'd like to take you there sometime."

I couldn't take in anything more than the reading I had just received. There was only one member of my family I needed to share it with. Outside my house, I leapt from Howard's car, barely saying goodbye, to get to the kitchen before everyone gathered for dinner. My mother had just placed frozen hamburger patties on a cookie sheet and was sliding them into a preheated oven.

"Emma, could you set the table?" Her tired face turned from the stove.

"Howard's friend was very interesting," I said to the uneven bow that secured my mother's apron. "She's a spiritualist medium."

Mom drew a long breath from her dwindling cigarette before setting it into her ashtray. I stepped up beside her, like a shadow, to open the silverware drawer.

"She said she had a message for me."

I placed a fork to the left of each melamine plate, with a folded napkin centered underneath. Mechanically, I positioned the knives and spoons, like I had done a thousand times before.

"She said she saw me sitting in a rocking chair," I went on, "and turning the pages of a book. She said I was holding Eddy."

When I spoke my brother's name, my mother turned around and stepped away from the stove. We sat down at the same time, in the same way, as if we were reflections of each other. With no related experience to draw from, she simply listened as I poured out the details of my most delicate and unexplainable meeting, feeling more emotionally connected to her than I ever had or ever would again.

CHAPTER 10

Wishes, Dreams, Responsibilities

Art classes had given me hope for a future. But even if I had outstanding grades, no college would consider me without a portfolio, my mother had discovered. Thankfully, for that very reason, a post-graduate art program had been designed.

Away from home, living with relatives, playing with other creative students who expressed themselves with fearless abandon, I had been thrust into fertile soil from which I could grow into my soul's desire. My hair soon fell in an asymmetrical style, half covering my dramatic eyes framed in dark liner that extended beyond the upper and lower lids.

"You look like a raccoon, Emma." My mother's single comment washed over me without a reply. Nothing would distract me from my metamorphosis, although it did take a bit longer than we all expected.

It was the gnawing need for perfection that struck hard and sent me running home for permission to quit the program and forget an art career altogether; that and one simple assignment with clear direction: "No pencils, no erasers, only ink."

I never would have imagined that a single assignment could inflict such fear. My ink drawing started at the center of the paper and drifted south into the lefthand corner like wind-blown snow, day after day, forcing me to face my mistakes and my inability to fix them. My carefully crafted oil paintings and a watercolor that would eventually receive an award had no value in the shadow of my dread of this class. I was humiliated to turn the artwork in for a grade and told myself this nightmare might someday become my fate.

"PLEASE, MOM," I BEGGED ON the weekend break. "I don't want to do this anymore."

"Emma, finish it out," my mother insisted, puzzled by my meltdown. "You're only weeks away from finishing."

On my final day, with every ounce of frustration, I dragged my pregnant portfolio from the car, up the two staircases, and across my bedroom floor to the closet, pushing it into the shadows where no reminder of my short-lived affair would be revealed. For three months I remained silent and brooding as my parents danced around me with an occasional, "What do you want to do, Emma?"

And then, the answer came. My frustrating inability to conceive a plan for my life ended in the flash of a moment. My true passion called a humane halt to my unbudging indecision. I made a critical U-turn.

The Springfield Dance Collective was a firmly established company with a budding teacher-training program. Dad was eager to enroll me. The classrooms were dark and empty when we arrived for my eleven a.m. appointment with Vincent Cosolino, the artistic director. Sitting behind his oversized desk in a windowless office, Vincent ran his fingers through his wavy brown hair and flashed a smile that seemed too large for his face.

"By four o'clock, all three studios are bustling with students," Vincent reported. He had pressed his long delicate fingers to his chest and opened his arms, holding them in the air in a position that I could see had taken years of training to become so natural. I chuckled at his entertaining choreography that embellished his explanation of the professional status of his dance company.

Pirouetting in his swiveling desk chair, he made his way around the room, pointing to every framed black and white photograph on his walls, boasting the talent of guest artists and faculty members, listing a variety of classes offered and performance opportunities for every age and achievement level. I felt I was home.

Within a few hours I had been accepted at The Dance Collective, had gotten a job at the Richmond Drugstore luncheonette, and was standing in the foyer of a rooming house practically across the street.

"Emma is a very responsible young lady," my father exclaimed, emphasizing *very* as he slid his arm around my waist and shoved me forward to display my upstanding nature. "Sam, at the drugstore, sent us to you."

"I only have male renters here." The landlady was repeating herself.

"Emma will be working at the drugstore luncheonette every morning." Dad was pointing at the large neon sign through the glass window in Mrs. Pelowski's storm door, "and she'll be taking classes at the dance school, right down the street, until eight at night. You'll hardly see or hear from her." My father's voice resonated with the soft tone he had learned to control and inflate in a way that left you asking to hear more. "All our daughters are very responsible." He smiled at the plump woman with a round face who had shuffled to the door in brown slippers with fur linings. She lifted the skirt of her apron and nervously wrung her dry hands as she reconsidered. He was pushing me toward the woman again. I looked to my father and back to her.

"This is a lovely home, Mrs. Pelowski," I obligingly broke the silence. "It would be so nice to be living here."

It all felt a bit fraudulent when Dad and I shook her hand one final time, to seal the deal. The rebel in me was already judging the *guarded spinster landlady*. How would she handle a twenty-year-old woman in her houseful of men? Mrs. Pelowski thanked my father for coming.

Pushed from the nest, I flew into the grueling schedule of work and dance that accelerated my transformation. With Vincent's prodding, my slightly pudgy and lazy frame lifted and shifted.

"All those years of bad technique, Emma," Vincent's words penetrated my most vulnerable places when he sauntered, unannnounced, into the beginner ballet class he had insisted I take. I had spent my final two years of "bad training" under the tutelage of an aging Russian ballerina who opened up a dance school half an hour away from our home, when I was a junior in high school. I don't think my mother ever had any formal ballet training. If she did, it never transferred to our classes in the pink basement. Mom's hand-sewn costumes were unique and beautifully crafted. Our experiences, on stage and off, were exciting and fun. I can say that the tap routines my mother pulled from books she ordered from a catalogue were detailed and interesting, but I can't say that we had any understanding of the meaning of "professional ballet technique."

Our recitals at the Grange hall, and in later years on the elementary school stage, couldn't compare to the professionally lit auditorium the Russian ballerina had access to. Unfortunately, the aging performer didn't have the patience to give us strong technical direction, but she fed my self-esteem, and had given me faith in my dream to become a professional dancer.

Here, at the Dance Collective, arduous, disciplined practice filled every moment in the classroom. Rehearsals ran throughout every weekend, when the Nutcracker ballet was drawing near. Even though I was only chosen to be a mother in the Prologue, it seemed I was always at the studio.

"Stick your stomach out," Vincent bellowed at an eight-year-old with pink bows in her hair who stood, petrified, beside me at my first rehearsal. His large dark eyes blatantly stared at my belly as she held her breath and pushed as hard as she could. The tiny girl couldn't inflate hers to the size of mine, sucked tightly to my spine. "Go ahead, honey, stick it out." Vincent always made his point.

When my auburn curls fell past my shoulders, the turnout in my well-defined legs and abnormally elevated arches had caused my feet to point almost sideways, wearing out the outer soles of my shoes. My belly had tightened like the head of a drum.

Suddenly I was running to rehearsals that flowed into the late night, performing on an enormous stage under warm spotlights in an elaborate theater with a full orchestra. No matter how insecure the little girl who used to dance in the basement felt on the inside, I was now grounded in my outer presence, moving with a physical confidence that reassured me: *Wherever life leads me I know I will always land on my feet.*

Kathleen tagged my cliffhanger-to-cliffhanger existence during those three years, from 1967 to 1969, a "soap opera." Almost proudly, I had agreed. I was an independent woman with an exciting life. Eviction from Mrs. Pelowski's roominghouse, sexual advances from my next landlord, the apartment eviction by my roommate and her mother, and my subsequent midnight arrival at the Springfield Y were only some of the dramatic stories I freely broadcasted. Like selected scenes from a long-running play, I enthusiastically told my tales. I seemed to be riding on the wave of turbulent times that had thrown the world around me into chaos.

When I walked through the Richmond Drug Store I saw the newspapers strewn across the counters of the luncheonette. Front-page spreads reported the assassinations of Martin Luther King and Bobby Kennedy, and the clashing beliefs we, as a country, were struggling with. College students were crouching over the back pages of their own newspapers, going through the names that were listed almost daily, it seemed, of those who had most recently been drafted into the Vietnam war. "Enlisted, against their will," we protested.

Young men fled to Canada. The graphic violence, riots, and bloodshed never before seen on television was relentlessly projected into our homes through the daily news. Although I was sheltered in rented rooms and dance studios, I was well aware. We were all glued to it, resisting it, wanting to change it.

"Peace, not war," we chanted. "Fuck the establishment," my friends began to repeat, in everyday conversations. "Power to the people," we were singing. "We shall overcome."

Legendary rock musicians were helicoptered in to Woodstock, the well-documented rock concert that jammed up major highways and drew a half million "hippies" to a six-hundred- acre farm in upstate New York, and became a "love-in." On our televisions we witnessed news clips of the four days of unprecedented music and peaceful cohabitation. This is what we wanted in the world, what we yearned for. Drugs that were pouring into the marketplace, labled "uppers" and "downers," were being passed around and experimented with. LSD was altering consciousness, offering experiences of spiritual enlightenment when it was a "good trip." Groups of people were moving in together in communes. The newly released birth control pill had hit the market. Women were burning their bras as a public statement that released them from old traditional restrictions, fortifying the growing women's liberation movement.

MY OWN PERSONAL FREEDOM FROM schedules at the dance collective perfectly aligned with the early summer opening of Mallory's, a new downtown bar my friends refused to go to without me. The live band, barely visible over the sea of gyrating silhouettes, drew me into the unrestricted energy that filled the dance floor. Oblivious to anything else, I allowed my sensual movements to ground and carry me forward in an ecstatic solo. I dropped my head, allowing

my long hair to sway across my chest. I waved for my friends to go
ahead. *Leave me here.*

The dark eyes that circled the room from the corner were calling
for consideration. It took me a while to notice. Casual glances grew
into interested smiles. Passion invited passion until he felt secure
enough to move in and introduce himself. "I'm Tony," he said.

Tony Di Fransesco became my main reason for returning to
Mallory's every night. His sense of humor drew me through the door
and into the group that consistently gathered around him. I stood
quietly at his table until I could get close enough to lean against his
back and slide my fingers through his black hair, the moment of
surprise that inevitably returned his eyes to mine.

His friends were artists and musicians who spent most of their
free time together. When we all sat privately, and talked about our
passionate concerns, the expected marijuana passed from hand to
hand and the word "man" was injected into every other sentence. "I
know, man. You're not kiddin', man."

I passed the joint along without touching my lips. Everyone was
"cool" with it. No judgment either way. I had made my choice of
abstinance after our recent date at an outdoor rock concert. Tony
had rolled two joints and we had smoked them before we arrived.
I was squeezing his hand and pulling him behind another couple
when we entered the gate and I caught sight of the cop who was
heading straight for us.

Tony yanked me back and patted the uniformed policeman
on the shoulder. "Hey, man." His lack of common sense sent me
"checking in" to be sure my confident posture was firmly grounded
in my black and white leather clogs.

"Emma, this is Norm, my brother-in-law." Tony smirked.

Oh, God. A great first impression.

I find it interesting, as I look back, that my foggy, short-lived
pot-smoking remembrances are more intact than those regarding

our initial sexual encounters. When we slid out of our clothes and I wrapped my legs around the man my soul could not resist, his familiar joking, which made everyone comfortable with Tony, erupted in our most personal moments. Surprisingly, after the pornography incident, my early sexual experiences turned out to be easy and comfortable, but I held an unconscious fear. My old unidentified trepidation over the risk of becoming a mature woman in my home had taken hold of me in a way I couldn't understand. Was I incapable, or unwilling, to step into a demonstrative, sexually seductive role?

Although Tony and I didn't have an immediate firey sexual connection, I craved his confident presence and his intimate connection to food. After every rehearsal, Tony picked me up, to be sure I had eaten, no matter what the hour. Tonight, as we exited the studio he walked beside me, my eyes drifting past the stars that held a brilliant light above us.

"Ansel was late," I could hardly wait to spill the news, "and Vincent was furious. When he finally stepped into the studio there was complete silence. I thought all hell would break loose right there." To punctuate my story, I opened the car door and threw my dance bag onto the back seat. "So, needless to say, the company took a break. We could hear those two yelling from the end of the hall."

Even in tights, my legs felt cold against the vinyl seats. I dropped my shoes to the floor and tucked my feet under my wool miniskirt.

"Ida came in and explained what had happened," I bubbled on. "Ansel was late because he had sent Ida to the drugstore for a box of Modess pads."

"Modess pads?" I had finally engaged Tony's curiosity.

"Yes, he uses them to pad his dance belt. Can you believe it? He wouldn't step into rehearsal without the padding."

It never occurred to me that Tony might not be interested in all the details surrounding the featured soloist from the New York City Ballet. Addiction to the drama had already kindled my next flame. "I heard that Ansel and Vincent are sleeping together."

My mindless chatter left no room for intimate conversation, and I had no idea how to do it differently. When I finally ran out of gossip, over dinner, there was a single moment when I noticed my fear of silence and sensed the subtle tugging in my stomach. "How's your mother?" I was desperate to keep a dialogue going.

"She's fine, Emma."

"How does she feel about our moving in together?"

"I haven't told her yet. I'm waiting until we find a place."

NOT ONLY AN APARTMENT WAITED in the wings. I found an abandoned second-floor dance studio calling for a fresh coat of paint and a new vision. With Tony's help, my latest dream was coming true.

"Where do you want this?" he yelled down from the open second-floor window, pressing the long metal bracket against the wooden shingles.

"That's perfect," I called back, adjusting the length of the chain on my hand-painted sign and heading up the stairs. Evolution Dance was about ready to open its doors.

In my new dance studio, I could smell the dust burning off the radiators as I raised the temperatures that pinked the cheeks of my pre-ballet students. "Don't forget to bring a sweater," I reminded them, "now that it's getting colder."

Bunched together like little chicks, they scurried to the wooden barres and spread out along them, each placing a tiny hand on the lower banister, locking their heels together like hinges and turning their toes outward. Taking a deep breath, I inhaled the love that circulated through them and returned to me. By some incredible stroke of fate I had found my place in the world.

CHAPTER 11

First Conscious Assessment

The sun sat on the horizon like a cantaloupe sliced down the center, revealing the juicy fruit inside its ordinary shell. I was staring out the window of a psychotherapist's office, a safe haven for those who were also lying open, ready to spill out. I was thirty-two years old, and had finally realized that I needed to talk to someone about what was going on in my life. When had I begun drinking vodka martinis and become capable of putting down an additional half bottle of wine over dinner? My unacknowledged emotions needed a voice, and the painful end of my marriage to Tony had pushed me to make this appointment.

"I'm Clarissa," the cheerful young woman with long brown hair greeted me, "and you must be Emma."

With chest lifted and legs turned out, I followed her to the room at the end of the hallway, on the right. She stood aside and allowed me to confidently lead her into her own office, as she observed me. I walked to her couch and slipped off my shoes, folding my legs under to sit comfortably on my feet. I moved a pillow to my side, plumped it, and sank my arm in the softness.

"So Emma, tell me, what has brought you here?" Clarissa's eyes sparkled through the large lenses of her tortoiseshell frames.

"A friend of mine referred me to your office. Gretchen Hall, a student of mine. She actually referred me to her therapist, but he wasn't available, so he referred me to you."

"And what brings you here?"

Where should I begin? There was so much to tell Clarissa. There had been too many overwhelming situations in nine fleeting years. I had pushed them down and denied the angry negative thoughts so I could keep on going and make everything fine.

Even now, as I prepare to write about the painful truths I was about to tell my therapist, a part of me insists on beginning with the sweet aroma of Tony's marinara sauce. It had seduced me that afternoon into the kitchen of our apartment, where I padded around in bare feet completely covered by the wide bellbottoms of my hip-huggers – my favorite pair of jeans, with a row of trim at the bottom and a star appliquéd at the right knee. Until I met Tony, I'd never been so aware of the sensual nature of eating. I was lifting the bowl of freshly grated romano cheese to my nostrils and breathing in. He was standing in front of the stove, enjoying the anticipation of tasting the infusion of red tomatoes, fresh garlic, and oregano. Everything he made exuded love.

This particular night Tony took his time serving up the chianti that always accompanied dinner. His black curls half covered his face as he leaned over the stemmed glasses and carefully poured. Taking one in each hand, he extended them both to me and waited until I chose.

"Will you marry me, Emma?" he asked, dropping to one knee and tapping our goblets together. I thought he was joking. "I'm serious," he said, tossing his head back to flick his hair from in front of his eyes. "I think we should get married."

I was waiting for his reason, but felt his urgent expectation. "We've been living together for over a year," he reminded. I placed my glass on the table and returned to his lingering question.

"You're sure you want to get married?"

"I have a friend who's a jeweler," he replied. Tony had a friend for everything.

Our vague conversation of questions and diversions concluded with me saying "yes." We promised to keep the sparkling yet imperfect diamond a secret until my approaching birthday.

IN THE TWO DAYS SEPARATING my father's birthday from mine, the configuration of stars shifts from Scorpio to Sagittarius. With each of us permanently seated on opposite banks of this astrological boundary line, Dad and I always celebrated together over Thanksgiving dinner. On this Thanksgiving, in 1971, Peg was wearing her own diamond solitaire. She and Doug had been friends since high school. I think they had agreed upon marriage before their junior prom. Their engagement was perfectly aligned with their upcoming college graduations.

Right before dinner Tony poured champagne and dropped my ring into the last glass. My heart resisted. For the first time I felt an upstaging of my younger sister's engagement, but it was too late.

"My dance school is just getting started," I reminded Tony as we sat at the foot of our bed that night. "What'll happen when we have children?"

"We'll deal with that when it happens," he said.

OUR DUAL ENGAGEMENTS BROUGHT ABOUT a meeting at Pine Ridge Country Club, our father's recent purchase, a nine-hole golf course in desperate need of repair. Nanny's sizable inheritance had granted my father this new start.

There wasn't one complaint from my mother when they moved out of the house and left behind all the memories and most of the furniture for Kathleen and Jon. A five-room apartment, attached to the broken-down clubhouse, now defined their converted life.

When Peg and I arrived at the club, Dad was pouring us drinks. "No, Dad," I held up my hand in an emphatic gesture. The cheap bourbon he always served had sent me home with a headache every time I had given in.

"You have to celebrate this special occasion," he insisted as he handed my mother her numbing midday cocktail. When she reached for it, I noticed the fleshy bags that had formed under her eyes. I had been caught up in my own life when she returned to college after twenty-three years of child-rearing. I was trying to get as far away from home as I could when she completed the remaining classes that expanded her associates degree to a bachelors. I clearly remember her struggling through the math classes. She pushed hard to finish in time to graduate with Kathleen, and by that time I was out of the house. But today, as I sat close to her, I could see that my mother's most recent challenge of taking on a full-time teaching job had increased her responsibilities to beyond manageable.

"A double wedding," my father proposed, scotch and soda hoisted as he placed the plan before us, "to save on the cost of doing everything twice." He nodded to my mother. She nodded back. "I'd love to sing *The Lord's Prayer* at your church service," he added.

Dad's offer was an unconscious seduction, to "sweeten the pot" he might have said. His mellow tenor voice had not only captured my mother's heart and soothed us when loved ones died. As the choir director at the Congregational church, he was revered for embellishing our Christmas parties with the voices of his choral angels as we gathered around Kathleen and our piano or electronic organ at the homestead.

"Your mother and I would like to send you on your honeymoons as a wedding gift." What more did we need to hear? Peg looked to me and our eyebrows rose. We could make it work. *Couldn't we?*

I imagined an outdoor wedding, casual, a wreath of flowers in my hair. Peg dreamed of a church wedding with cathedral trains and the *Trumpet Voluntary*. We would make it work.

Peg, Doug, Tony, and I went through bottles of wine as we mulled over books of wedding invitations. They could get a deal on the band. We agreed to pay for the flowers. Kathleen offered to make both of our gowns and, thanks to our mother's teaching, had the expertise to do so. We had everything but the meal covered.

PEG WAS BUSY WITH HER college finals, so I agreed to meet our parents at the restaurant, to make our reception arrangements. I remember it being an unusually warm day that forced me to change into a lightweight cotton blouse. Mom stepped out of her car in a crisp beige shirtwaist dress covered with tiny aqua flowers. Shirtwaist dresses were her everyday attire. She always wore them with flat-soled sneakers and short white socks. Today she had put on nylon stockings and a pair of beige flats. Her short brown hair was tightly curled from a recent perm and she had applied bright red lipstick.

As she stepped out of the driver's seat, I didn't ask where Dad was. The golf course, like the funeral home, had become his priority. I immediately realized that my mother was not in a mood to discuss the excitement of our upcoming double wedding. I could feel the seriousness of the business we were about to take care of. It was that same, serious, *just get it done* energy I had felt every time she had piled my sisters and I into the car and taken us grocery shopping with her. We went every couple of weeks, and always filled two carriages with cans of assorted vegetables, pasta, tuna fish, powdered milk, eggs, Wonder Bread, and frozen hamburger patties. With Dad's unreliable income, my mother always asked the clerk at the register to add the total of our purchase to a running tab. Today, my mother was not only making arrangements to feed everyone. I soon understood that this time she was also carrying the personal responsibility of paying for it.

She tapped her short nails on the linen tablecloth as she listened to our menu options. I watched the tears well in her eyes as she was given the final tally for the roast chicken dinners and champagne toast. Tony's family was three times larger than ours, and his mother had insisted on inviting everyone, even the children. The familiar ache in my belly held tight to the unexpressed feelings I didn't have words for. I didn't know how to say, "I'm sorry this is so hard for you, Mom," or "Why isn't Dad here to share the responsibility with you?" All the questions that come up now, as I think back, were mere unsprouted seeds then, which I was unable to verbally express. My mother departed as unobtrusively as she had arrived.

It seemed I was always the one who witnessed my mother's pain and felt her suffering. Certainly, no one was aware of the confrontation I had observed only months before, after her recent stay at the hospital for acute chest pain. Her weekly paycheck hadn't released her from my father's demands. From April to November she cooked hamburgers and french fries at Pine Ridge every afternoon. Her belief that she was expected to do it all had brought forth, for as long as I could remember, the martyr in her.

Pericarditis was my mother's diagnosis, a potentially serious condition that required an extended period of rest. When Dad and I arrived at the hospital to take her home, she looked pale as she sat on the bed, dressed and waiting. As we walked to the car she sighed, a habit she had developed over the years. I sighed along with her. From the back seat I could see she was unsettled. She kept changing positions.

"I'm not supposed to do any work for a week, Ed. Dr. Matthews said not for a week." He remained silent, but she was not going to let my father ignore her this time. "It's important to take things slow while I recuperate."

"It's not life-threatening, Sarah. We have a banquet this weekend, and I need you to work."

My hands clenched the seat.

"I'm not supposed to work," she repeated, weakly. "I can't work."

"It's just an inflammation! It's not your heart, it's the tissue around your heart, and you can work on Saturday night."

My mother gasped, her fragile body falling forward as she burst into tears.

"Dad!" I yelled into the back of his head. "Pull the car over!"

He slammed on the brakes and drove onto the soft grass with my mother pressed up against the window, releasing the short breaths of an injured animal. He became a statue with a face that had been chiseled into an angry thought. We sat frozen until his voice broke the tension. "I'm sorry, Sarah. I'm sorry if I upset you."

I had never heard him raise his voice to her. Like the searing burn of a branding iron, this intimately painful image imprinted itself in my mind. There was nothing more I could say or do. On Saturday night, she worked.

CLARISSA LOOKED UP FROM HER notepad and responded to the last thing I had said to her, about my dance school just getting started and my concerns about caring for a family. "So, Emma, you and Tony never discussed your joint vision of marriage and children?"

"No," I admitted.

I wasn't going to leave the office without telling my therapist about the crucial moment. The missed opportunity. This is the part I was irritably ready to tell. "He wasn't the least bit serious about a long-term commitment."

On that afternoon I was counting the days until our wedding, exactly twenty-one. Tony returned from work with hot-fudge sundaes, and I dropped what I was doing to grab mine. I tore off the domed lid so I could see the merging of cooling chocolate and warming whipped cream. I couldn't wait another second to slip my plastic spoon into the sweet melting. He took his time coming into the living room, seating himself on our recently purchased second-hand couch, leisurely opening the white bag and reaching in. He deliberately placed his covered wax cup at the center of the ottoman, pushed himself back in his seat, directly across from me, and waited for my gaze to lift from the sweetness.

"When I left work today I stopped at the diner," he said. Tony often stopped at his uncle's diner for lunch. "Becky was coming out from her shift."

Becky was the new waitress.

"She's been working part time," he explained.

Tony's hands were clasped as he leaned forward and rested his elbows on his knees. Underneath his irrelevant comment ran a current of uncertainty. The early July heat flooded the apartment, encouraging me to take my final spoonful of ice cream.

"We took a ride and talked and," I already knew. "We made out for a long time."

My spoon scratched along the softening empty bottom of the paper cup. I was digging for an appropriate response. My thoughts were barely audible. *Don't say anything. There's nothing you can do about it without upsetting everyone.*

"It didn't mean anything, Emma." My eyes shifted from the empty cup I now held in my hands to the meltdown that sat before us.

"Are you going to eat that?" I stared at his untouched sundae.

He rolled his eyes and shook his head.

I traded cups, gripping my plastic spoon like a weapon, scooping the lukewarm soup into my mouth. Behind my averted eyes, the strands of tension pulled taut between us, hot glass stretched to its limit.

"How can you listen to what I'm telling you and, and eat?" His arms were waving. He shot off the couch and began pacing in front of me.

Years of "shutting down" at family meals had taught me well. I placed the half-empty container into its empty mate and gathered the courage to look Tony in the eyes. Undomesticated rage blew my shell wide open, exposing the vulnerable creature inside.

"How could you do this?" My words grew into an earsplitting scream as I grappled with the ring that wouldn't budge over a swollen knuckle. I tore it from my finger and flung the flawed diamond through the doorway. The shining symbol of promised commitment skimmed the scuffed linoleum, coming to rest underneath the washing machine. I ran up the stairs and locked myself in the bathroom. Twenty-three years of tears poured into my hands.

When I emerged, Tony was sitting at the end of our bed with the ring in his hand. I sat down beside him without comment. Our wedding was three weeks away. I could see no options. To an offering of open arms and an unconvincing smile I closed my eyes and selectively deleted the last hour and a half of my life. Everything would go on as planned.

"You couldn't find a way to get out of the commitment, Emma?" Clarissa stepped back in. "There was no one you could talk to about this?"

"No one."

CHAPTER 12

Betrayals

In my rented condo I hung over the teakettle, as still as a stone, but my relentless thoughts were running at full speed. I had already mentally reviewed my first therapy appointment, and now I was lining up the facts, trying to make sense of how I came to be standing here in this moment, with eyes glassed over, one hand resting on the rounded handle as I waited for the familiar whistle.

We had vacationed in Bermuda on our honeymoon. Tony had purchased the tickets, knowing my father was going to renege on his original offer to pay. Things seemed to be going well for us after that. He took photographs of my dancers. I wrote press releases and dropped the formal packets off at the local newspapers. He joined a softball league and I followed him to games and related events. As our families grew, we fell into the flow of it. The Thanksgivings, the Christmases, the Fourth of July picnics, and all of the birthdays. Life carried us, and as it did, Tony became more and more distant. Peg had given birth to her third child. Kathleen had two. I hadn't been able to get pregnant, and I was pushing Tony to think about adoption, but he avoided those conversations. Three nights a week I worked at my school, and from April to June I was rehearsing every weekend, in preparation for our spring concert.

Building a home and moving in next door to our best friends felt like an ideal situation. From the time I met Roger and Rochelle

I had felt close to them, and I adored their two young daughters. Yvonne was a smart, sensitive child who would choose to sit and read or tell you what she had learned over practically anything. Giselle was older, more creative, and much more energetic. She was tall, even when she was ten, and started taking classes with me the following year. In five years she had become one of my best dance company members, and the summer that we decided to build on the lot next door to them, Giselle asked me if she could teach one of my pre-ballet classes. Finally, she was ready to take on the responsibility.

Roger was one of those meticulously perfect carpenters, the one you would hire in a second, and he was eager to help us out in every way, to make my dream home become a reality. To find the perfect design, I went through every available house plan magazine. Tony generously handed me a credit card, encouraging me to choose whatever rugs and fixtures I desired. He borrowed money from my father without my knowing and expanded the ranch plan to a colonial. We added an entire floor (that we planned to finish in the years ahead), to increase the "in-law options" and "resale value." Before the living room flooring had been ordered we moved in. Two months later, Tony walked out.

"IT ACTUALLY SERVED HIM THAT I didn't make a lot of money," I grumbled into the phone when Gina called a few months later. "He used me as a tax write-off." I had finally found the courage to look at my seemingly insurmountable predicament, and I was making a feeble attempt at justifying my financial situation. My husband was brilliant in his ability to make money, and every year when we sat with our accountant and gave him the final figures for our tax returns, Tony always made a point of embarrassing me about how little I made. The accountant insisted that our tax return was higher because of it, but Tony still tried to talk me into selling photographs of my students and expensive pre-made costumes at a large mark up, to increase my "bottom line." I stubbornly told him that this was ethically wrong. I truly believed it was.

Gina remained patient with me as I ranted at her. She wanted to help by letting me get it out of my system. "I know this has been hard for you," she finally interjected, ready to turn my depressing conversation in a more uplifting direction. Home from college for the summer, she was staying with Katheen and Jon. "But you need a day off, and the pool's open."

"Dad's coming on Saturday, for a 'talk'" I sighed.

"Oh," her voice deflated.

"I've missed two mortgage payments, Gina. My electric bill has been costing as much as my mortgage."

"Would you like me to be there?" She paused, and so did I. "When he comes to the house, would you like me to be there with you, as support?"

"That would be great."

On Saturday morning Gina and I sat in my kitchen, staring into the wooded acres that shaded every room of my house. We had nothing urgent to talk about. We were waiting and listening for the sound of tires rolling up the long dirt drive.

I don't remember hugging my father, although I'm positive I did. Once I opened the door and let him in, it was all business. My sister and I sat together at my own kitchen table feeling like children again, as he began assessing the oak cabinets and the stonework in the sunken family room.

"I can't believe Tony's done this," I stood to communicate my grievance to my father, "left me in this house, on my own."

Dad turned from us and walked into the empty front rooms, nearly bumping his head on the unlit chandelier.

"Where's he going?" I hissed at Gina, through clenched teeth. "Why isn't he listening to me?"

My sister lifted her long blonde hair away from her downturned face. Her blue eyes rose to meet mine. My father reentered the room and calmly explained the steps I should take to sell the house. I agreed to it all.

"He couldn't even stay in the room with me," I complained to Aunt Rae when she called from Florida a few days later.

"Emma," Aunt Rae confided, "he can't talk about what's happening to you. Your father wasn't faithful to your mother."

Confirmation of the suspicion I had carried for years, that my father was not only capable of having affairs, but had actually had one, sent me reeling to the edge of my bed. I immediately thought of the afternoon Harriet, a member of the church choir Dad had once directed, came to the golf course with her two-year-old son. "This is Eddy," she said, with a childish smile. My mother didn't come out of the apartment to acknowledge Harriet's visit, and I had never said a word to her about my mounting questions which had begun years before, on the nights Dad dropped me off to babysit for Harriet's daughter so Hariett could accompany him to choir rehearsals. Those late nights, far beyond rehearsal hours, had been briskly explained away.

I thought he might have even had a second secret relationship, when he was out of town, working for another funeral home, but I didn't ask Aunt Rae who the other woman was. I hoped it was only one. As if my voice had been mortally wounded by my own knowing, I withdrew from our conversation, placed the receiver back on the hook, and curled up under the sheets.

"That bastard!" I screamed into my pillow. "Why didn't you speak up for yourself and leave him, Mom? He destroyed you!"

I was engulfed in the memory of the apartment Tony and I had left for our new home, and the living room couch where my mother had rested on her last visit. She had shown us the lesion she found on her breast, which she was now being treated for.

"Mom's been admitted to the hospital," Kathleen calmly announced, when she called to deliver the latest news. Tony and I had been drinking wine and looking at house plans. Frost had gathered on our windows and a brisk wind was blowing the dry November leaves across our backyard. My hand tightened on the phone as my sister's controlled voice continued, "but it's pneumonia, Emma. At least it's not the cancer." Naiveté and denial barricaded us from the truth. "Gina's in the middle of her finals and she'll be home for Thanksgiving, so we're going to wait to tell her."

When I arrived at the hospital I pleaded with the nurse for assistance, but the ventilator seemed more of a discomfort than a help. Kathleen rubbed her hands together to warm the lotion she tenderly applied to Mom's feet. When I touched them, they felt ice cold.

"I'm going to take Sarah to Hawaii when she's released," Dad explained to the patient on the other side of the thin curtain that separated us from them. While my sister and I watched our mother struggle for air, he moved closer to the patient he didn't know. "Sarah loves Hawaii."

It was a few days later when Gina touched down at the airport and Dad picked her up. The doctor had given my mother a few days, at best. In two days it would be Thanksgiving. Gina was full of anticipation about all the festivities. Dad couldn't tell her that her mother was dying. She had no idea what awaited her. She dropped off her bags at my parents' apartment and changed her clothes before they headed for the hospital. Kathleen and I wouldn't be there for another few hours.

When Gina reached out to hug our mother and realized conversations were no longer possible, no one was with her. She had no one to support her when she realized the truth. No matter how close Dad physically stood, he was miles away from emotionally present as she tried to make sense of the nightmare she had come home to.

WHILE KATHLEEN AND JON PREPARED the turkey and all the trimmings in the warm surroundings of our comfortable homestead, Tony and I made the trip from our apartment in frigid silence. He pushed the buttons on the car radio, looking for a song that would entertain him. I stared into the long road ahead.

Before making his announcement, he turned the volume all the way down. It took me a moment to take in what he was saying. "I've been having an affair, Emma." Without hesitation he had exchanged one gut-wrenching emotional drama for the other. "With Paige," he added after a long pause. *The bank teller who always waits on me. She's the one who called two separate times and hung up when I answered the phone.* I couldn't access another thought. Tony knew there would be no recourse.

On this Thanksgiving we didn't open any birthday gifts. After a solemn dinner we all headed for the hospital, where I spent the evening of my thirtieth birthday by my mother's side, intently focused on how she was going to die.

Tony didn't offer a word of comfort that night. I drifted into a hollow sleep, then woke into darkness. The digital clock read 4:05. My eyes refused to close. I lay awake for nearly an hour before my father's call.

"Your mother has died, Emma." His voice was calm. "I'd like you girls to meet me here at noon."

WRAPPED IN RAW, UNACKNOWLEDGED EMOTION, the circle of sisters gathered in our parents' living room to discuss funeral arrangements. Dad read the obituary he had just written, then placed it on his lap. The statement he was about to make stands out with incredible clarity because he had boasted so often about being an atheist. It was his love of music and the cash payment, not his reverent beliefs, that had caused him to become the choir director at the Congregational church. I had assumed that his not believing in God, and being able to find every contradiction in the Bible, meant a lack of any spirituality, but he took me aback with his announcement.

"Your mother came to me last night," he said, "to say goodbye." My eyes opened wide at the thought.

"I woke up at five after four," I told him.

"She came to me at four o'clock." Kathleen's voice startled me. We looked at each other and then to the remaining two.

"I was restless and got up for a glass of water around four," Peg admitted. Gina had slept through.

This was one of the experiences that made my father impossible for me to understand. When he sang at church, I believed every word he was singing. When company arrived he was charming. Now, he believed in spirits connecting after death. For me, this was deliciously seductive. I felt, in this moment, that he was deeper than we knew him to be, and his vulnerability opened a space for me to love and trust him again.

THE DAY AFTER MOM'S BURIAL, at Dad's request, the four of us took another trip to our parents' apartment. I was the last one in, probably the most reluctant to go through the personal belongings I had never folded or sorted. Kathleen had reached the living room when I felt the discomfort rippling through the others, bringing us all to a halt. A sense of urgency pushed me to double my steps and see for myself what kept my sisters from entering.

The redheaded woman placed her scotch and soda on the coffee table, then turned to say hello.

"Hello, Harriet," Kathleen spoke for us, as no explanations were offered and, with his familiar detachment, Dad diverted us into the bedroom.

"Can you believe she's here?" My teeth were clenched again. Peg and Gina had worked at the golf course for three summers. I was sure I wasn't the only one who knew about Harriet's visits, and her son, who had been given my father's name, but they ignored me and stood united in the task in front of them. I was not going to extract one word of acknowledgment of what might be going on in the next room.

Although I never saw Harriet again, I did store this revealing final moment with all the other memories I was committedly collecting. In a family reluctant to express any pain or suffering, I seemed to be carrying it all and dragging with it an inescapable truth: Betrayals I continually witnessed and judged in my father, and had tried to run away from, had now played out in my own marriage.

CHAPTER 13
Beneath The Surface

I sat over my bills in my rented condo, deciding which were the most important to pay first. I was managing well, on my own, a year and a half into my move from the house. Tony knew he was leaving when he placed the mortgage in Dad's hands. My father had been generous enough to give me a small sum of money, a "nest egg," he called it, on the day my house was sold. It had given me the means to take the step into therapy.

I agreed to see Clarissa every week. When I eventually ran out of stories, she took out a chalkboard and drew diagrams that were meant to explain the different dynamics of my family. *She's younger than me, just out of school,* I imagined, as I became bored with her presentations. I wondered, as I walked up the stairs of my spacious condo, if I would be seeing her for much longer.

I gathered enough leotards and tights for a couple of loads of laundry and lifted them into my arms to take them downstairs to the washing machine. The door was closed to the spare bedroom. I rarely went in there. I had jammed more furniture in that room than I could have ever imagined, piece against piece, boxes crammed into the remaining spaces, stuff I couldn't part with but had no room to use. The rest was neatly piled as "temporary storage" in Kathleen's attic.

I couldn't worry about things that couldn't be changed. I walked through my day like all the others, with a strong agenda that kept me moving. Until I slipped into my tiny pink nightgown and slid into bed, my thoughts kept me focused.

When my mind stilled enough, and I nearly fell off to sleep, a new choreographic sequence sailed into my mind. Music I had already chosen filled my head, lifting me out from under the covers and across the room, where the jazz album sat ready to be played. *Five-six-seven, step-leap, contract to the floor.* My rhythmic dance flowed through the playful child that wanted to be bounced on someone's knee. There was no room for depression here, only joy in my ability to rebound as I continued leaping, rolling, and sitting crosslegged, scribbling my ideas on an empty envelope. In the morning I transferred my creative station to the kitchen, where I sat over a strong cup of tea and allowed my ambitious hands to doodle costume designs on slips of paper strewn across the table.

"You have an artistic temperament," my mother used to say. More often I wondered what that meant. All of my sisters showed artistic capabilities, so why was I chosen for this particular label? The "temperament" part is what caused me to question.

One afternoon, just before my sixteenth Christmas, my mother attempted to explain. She had strolled up the attic stairs and taken a seat on the bench along the half-wall partition between Kathleen's bedroom and mine. Rarely making her way to the third floor, she caused me to wonder if I'd done something wrong.

"We just got a card from your Uncle Martin," Mom said. "Your father hasn't heard from him in years, but he sent us this card and I thought you might like to see it."

The simple ink sketch of a road winding along snow-covered hills didn't inspire much interest, except where the evergreens stood with heavy white branches. "Merry Christmas" was written across the bottom in a bold and creative hand.

"He made it himself," my mother explained.

"It's nice," I said.

"He's an artist, like you, Emma. Your Uncle Martin draws and paints and writes editorials for his local newspaper."

"Where does he live?"

"Wyoming," she said, waiting patiently for my response as I turned the card over and stared into its unprinted back. I was wondering whether I had ever met my father's brother. Somehow I knew there had been a rift between them along the way.

"May I keep it?"

"Yes, I think he'd like you to have it."

I waited for the sound of her footsteps to reach the bottom of the stairs before I pulled the cushion from the bench and lifted the hinged lid. Beneath my unused diary was a shoe box half filled with personal treasures I hadn't shared with my sisters or even my best friend, Vicky. On that afternoon I placed Uncle Martin's card inside and promptly forgot about it.

I HAD NO THOUGHTS OF my uncle this morning, as I took the last sip of tea and gathered my own drawings from the kitchen table in anticipation of a scheduled creative afternoon with Kathleen. All she needed was a rough sketch and a basic pattern to bring my costumes to life. When I stepped into her dining room with two giant bags of fabric, she lifted her shears and waved them across the fully opened table that had finally been returned to the downstairs. "It looks like we have our work 'cut out' for us," she chuckled.

I sniffed the air as I pulled out the folded pink chiffon and ran my hand across a wrinkle, pushing it to the outer edge. "Did you bake?" I asked, knowing she had.

"Almond puff pastry," she winked, knowing it was one of my favorites. "I wrote out a recipe card for you. Don't forget to take it."

The sweet aroma was already drawing me back to the afternoon I had come to Kathleen for advice, shortly after Tony had moved out. As we began pinning from opposite ends of the table I started telling my sister about this sensual connection to another afternoon over almond puff pastry.

Kathleen had been exceptionally focused that day. I think she was hoping to change the outcome of the inevitable. She offered the name of a woman I had met at family picnics and neighborhood gatherings. I had no idea Kathleen's friend was an astrological counselor.

"Analise has really helped us," my sister had explained. "She's done astrological readings for Jon, the kids, and me over the years. She can draw up charts for you and Tony, to give you a sense of what you're dealing with. She'll make suggestions about how you might move toward a solution together."

Her idea could at least open up a conversation between Tony and me, I had considered. *He's met Analise and might be willing to sit through an appointment separate from mine.*

My hand was chilled from the April rain when I rang Analise's doorbell. She offered a seat by a little space heater with glowing red coils. I slipped out of my new espadrilles and crossed my legs in the deep-cushioned chair, tucking my bare toes under my warm body. Analise presented me with a chart that she had drawn by hand according to the placement of the planets at the exact date and time of my birth. I didn't realize how unique that concept was. She had only recently begun illustrating in this creative way to make it easier for her clients to comprehend. I was immediately drawn into the colorful intersecting lines that ran across a large circle, connecting the zodiac signs in a way that formed a clear central configuration.

"You see, Emma," she said, "this is a bowl, and it's pouring out. Your chart represents a personal mandala of your life. The blue lines signify areas where there's no friction. Everything moves freely, like a waterwheel. Red lines take adjustment and compromise. Yellow shows us where energy is always available to you. Green lines signify internal conflict."

Complicated, I thought. "Why am I represented as a bowl?"

"The upturned bowl shows you're being filled with the readiness to empty out. There's something you need to spill out to other people," she explained. "It's important to you that it's original and unique. And, it must have personal meaning.

"There are two themes in your life, my friend: the need for freedom and individuality, and the need for security and practicality." I imagined these two themes might be represented in the green-line category of internal conflict. I turned my attention back to the chart.

"You come to me with the problem of relationship, Emma. Your chart shows me that you are looking for one that's unique and gives you a lot of freedom." She tilted her head down and looked at me over her glasses. "What you need may not be conventional.

"As you've become more confident, you've become the director of a beautiful dance school and not 'the wife.' Tony had different expectations. I know you've been trying to get pregnant; having children feels important to you. But in this lifetime your soul has chosen to make a name for yourself and test yourself in the public eye. This is not always possible with children.

"You and Tony have charts that complement each other by being almost opposite," she went on. "You fill each other's empty areas but lack balance on your own. A mutual tendency to be brutally honest causes power struggles. You are willing to work in relationships, Emma, because of your earth connections. Tony doesn't have strong earth connections."

Analise shifted her papers under the bright light of her gooseneck lamp. She was rereading her notes to be sure of her wording.

"Even without the relationship issue, you need to look at the fact that you have internal tension." I looked back into the dark-green lines. "Tony's chart, as well as yours, shows the beginning of something and the end of something. As you know, Tony has already met with me. He isn't sure what he's going to do."

It was another week before Tony arrived to share our joint astrological readings. He hadn't brought along his mandala chart. He opened the cupboard, poured himself a double scotch, and set it on the kitchen table before excusing himself to go to the bathroom. An ice cube cracked in the frosted glass. Tony had positioned his unfolded wallet beside his drink. I picked it up to bring the exposed picture close enough so I could read the inscription: *yours forever, Giselle.*

Giselle. The suspicion I prayed was not true. I had taught her to be confident and strong. I had trusted her with my most precious dancers. She had sent me Mother's Day cards I saved in my shoe box. Tony knew this piece of evidence would nail her to the wall like a bounty hunter's reference and turn the attention away from him. I flew to the bathroom, where within seconds my rage anihilated any possibility of redemption. The pain of it was my impetus to find a lawyer and move on.

I LEFT MY CONDO A little early, to give myself plenty of time to get to my next appointment with Clarissa. She was standing in the doorway, waiting for me when I arrived. The chalkboard had been put away and she had moved her chair from behind her desk and placed it closer to the center of the room.

"So, Emma, how was your week?" she asked as I looked at her through curious eyes.

It's possible I really didn't want to talk about any more stories. Maybe it was the change of seating that shifted Clarissa's focus. She spoke more softly, intentionally. Like a shepherdess gathering her sheep, she herded my external thoughts closer together and directed them back into myself. The "charge" I usually felt dropped away. My mind became still and I noticed I was staring into an open space. I had slowly and unknowingly entered the garden of my unconscious, and underneath the bleeding hearts and bittersweet, the overgrown vine of abandonment that had flourished since childhood stood strong. Overwhelming emotions began to find words.

"I feel sad," I said. "In being discarded, I mean. I'm not any different than I ever was. What did I do wrong to cause him to leave?" I began picking at my perfectly manicured nails. "How could he just leave me?"

In the tidal wave of emerging feelings and questions I had never articulated, I barely noticed Clarissa looking at the clock.

"He never said anything about leaving," I continued.

The nail of her index finger was tapping on the glass face of her watch. She gently interrupted. "We need to come to closure for today, Emma. We can continue with this next week."

"Next week?"

"I have a luncheon engagement at noon. We need to wrap up our session," she explained.

You don't have another few minutes to hear what I'm telling you? I screamed inside my head. "Next week?" I asked again.

"Next week, same time." She was narrating her own script as I was making plans to do otherwise.

Never! I silently yelled back at her as she escorted me to the front door.

Pouring rain fused the cut neckline of my sweatshirt to my skin as I stomped across the parking lot. With every turn of the steering wheel, scenery passed by me like a silent movie. I burst through the front door of my condo and stormed up the stairs. Like a snowflake falling on a warm hand, my breakthrough moment had been lost.

"Betrayer!" I bellowed, fisting my hands at thoughts of my father and Tony. "I'm finished with therapy." My thunderous voice sent my cat into the spare bedroom. I followed her to make amends, but my intuition was suddenly directing my every move. *There's something I'm in here for,* I realized.

I leaned against a chair that had been turned upside down on a desk. *Where did I put it?* I had carried that raggedy shoe box with me everywhere, tightly cinched with a broad elastic band. With fired-up determination I unstacked the pile of corrugated boxes in front of the closet, opened the door, and dove in for the relief of finding it.

My heart raced as I dropped to the floor, relentless fingers scratching at the elastic band until it sprang across the room. I tore open the cover of the little gray box and shook out its contents. All the prominent memories scattered before me: the Mother's Day card with Giselle's flowery handwritten expressions, the angry note Tony nailed to the garage door after I changed the locks, and the picture taken at Vicky Weldon's wedding, where Tony and I stood coupled like Sonny and Cher. Sitting with my legs stretched, I revisited the confetti mix of memorabilia I had thrust onto the stained carpet... both the pain and the joy.

When I scooped it all up to put it away, the familiar ink sketch fell to the floor, evergreen side up, hooking and reeling me back to my third-floor bedroom and my mother's intentional visit. *Maybe,* I thought, *my dramatic life is more connected to Uncle Martin than I know.*

CHAPTER 14

Opportunities Knock

Our November birthdays were being celebrated at Margaret's that year. We all loved her from the start, before she became Dad's constant companion and an expected guest on holidays. When he moved into her home, balance returned to our family.

Margaret's smile broadened as she met me at her front door. Usually the last to arrive, I felt conspicuously early.

"Emma!" Dad shouted from the living room. "We're in the second quarter."

I shook my head and Margaret gave me a hug, pausing to hang my jacket in the closet before disappearing into the kitchen. I turned toward the sounds of sportscasters, whistles, and cheering fans. He didn't divert his eyes from the screen as I took my seat and asked, "Who's playing?"

"Notre Dame and Penn State. It's gonna be close."

My hand reached into the bowl of cashews that were connected to football like Christmas to decorations, birthdays to cakes. He raised his cigar and paused before it reached his lips.

"NO!" he bellowed, nearly startling the nuts from my cupped hand. "That was out of bounds. Come on…"

I sat respectfully until a string of commercials allowed him to break from the action and turn his attention my way. "Dad," I said. I knew time was limited, so I got right to the point. "I've been

Jan Johnson

thinking about Uncle Martin." He uncrossed his legs and recrossed with the other leg on top. "I found one of his Christmas cards a few weeks ago and I've been thinking of calling him. I wonder if you'd be willing to give me his number."

"Let me see if I have it," he said, as he placed his hands on the arms of his recliner, pushed himself to an upright position, and headed for the bedroom. Beneath the rousing Pepsi commercial I could feel my anxious heart thumping with anticipation.

He returned holding a notecard with a red rose on the front, obviously the first bit of paper he had been able to find in Margaret's desk. "I don't have a phone number," his eyes looked authentically apologetic, "but here's an address. We haven't been in touch for a while. I imagine your Uncle Martin still lives here." His willing hand extended the answer to my request, holding it in the air before me.

I grabbed it, fearing that he still might renege, then hesitated in the thought that I had been impolite. He didn't seem to have detected my desperation. The cigar stub that had gone out in the ashtray was already back in his hand. He was lighting a match underneath its tip. I slipped the card into my purse as I watched him draw the smoke through his lips and blow it into the air. The gray cloud expanded and dissipated as I sat in the familiar smell.

THE NEXT MORNING I STARED into my father's writing like a fortune-teller waiting for advice from beyond. When I felt ready I placed my hand on the phone, slowly lifted the receiver, and dialed Information. I jotted down the number, wiped the counter, put in a load of laundry, and finished a yogurt before summoning the courage to make the call. My eyes fell again on the blooming rose.

"Hello?" A cheery voice broke into my wordless wandering. I leaned forward on the chair as if it would lessen the distance between us.

"Uncle Martin, this is your niece Emma. Ed's daughter."

"Well, hello, Emma." There wasn't a second of hesitation. My locked posture softened to his openness.

"I have a Christmas card of yours," I said. "You designed it quite a few years ago, and my mother gave it to me because she said I was a lot like you, an 'artistic temperament,' she said." My words raced along with my thoughts, trying to get it all out. "I was hoping you might be willing to write to me and we could connect."

"Certainly, Emma!" Uncle Martin's enthusiasm was contagious.

I promised to write soon.

My dance school brochure, our latest newsletter, and a box of stationery sat on the table before me as heat rose in my hand with every committed stroke. Not a word was rethought or challenged. It was simply... time. When I finally slipped the overstuffed, double-stamped envelope into the mailbox, I triumphantly raised the little red flag.

December 5, 1982

My dear devotee of dance and niece Emma,

What to say in answer to your packet of goodies and delightful letter? It was music to my ears that a birthday gathering of the Edward Morgan family opened the way for a new relationship between an uncle and an unknown niece.

Ah, the days of childhood when our parents explain who we are and why this is so. In answer to your first question, yes, your great grandmother was a full blooded Sioux Indian. It was a great secret we were taught to keep. I find your revelation a gratifying moment of accepting the diversity of your rich heritage.

As for your creative ancestry, I can think of no other reason for your Mom to say "the creative talents come from the Morgan side of the family," than perhaps she felt she did not possess them in herself. I will attest to the fact, however, that they thrive on our side.

Your Grandma was quite dramatic and loved to sing. This is where your father discovered his voice. Your "artistic temperament" is a natural inheritance you have been blessed with, my dear.

The "rocky period" you have heard about that kept your parents from seeing or speaking to me went far beyond "rocky". It was wrecking and brought about the split. After all those vacant years, I'm thankful that the mysterious uncle is no longer absent. I'm pleased to know that our talking over the phone was a wish fulfilled.

Please excuse my hunt and peck typing. My old hands prefer it to long hand these days. And, speaking of long hand, I must say that your penmanship indicates the flare, grace, and very soul that lies within you.

THE VERY SOUL THAT LIES WITHIN YOU. My eyes teared as I considered the energy my mother couldn't articulate, the creative sensitivity that drove me to be free of convention. I had finally connected with a family member who not only recognized me but could clearly describe what he saw.

Uncle Martin's next delivery was a larger, more complex version of the handmade card I kept in the shoe box. Folded inside was an eight by eleven inch copy of a recent photograph he had scanned and enlarged at a print shop. The early technology had created a blurry rendition, but I could make out the essence of my uncle's face, whose shadowed eyes seemed to survey me from underneath the brim of his large cowboy hat. I quickly sat down with a glass of wine and my favorite stationery to reply.

WITH RENEWED EXCITEMENT I BEGAN packing up my belongings once again. A four-room cottage on Congamond Lakes was available for half my condo rent. With winter winds howling I could already visualize sitting at the lake in the warmer months and feeling the calming shift that always happened when I was near the water. In a few days I would be picking up the key to the affordable space that needed a lot of work. My new landlord had given me permission to make updates before I moved in.

"Four moves ago," I reminded myself as I pushed the lightweight summer bedspread deeper into the box and dropped my hand-sewn pink and lavender satin pillows on top. "I made these when Tony and I moved into our apartment, four moves ago."

December 29, 1982

Dear Emma,

There are so many things to learn about you. The many years of absence are like a long lost jewel that has been discovered in a dusty corner. I'm regenerated in its retrieval.

Glad to hear you were over a glass of white wine and not under it! Wine was not my drink. Whiskey was the power and glory. Ah, that good old I W Harper, 100 proof. Now, twenty-six years buried and forgotten, it's like a bad dream.

It seems to me that your new venture, the small cottage, will help fill the void and cover past grief. Your February performances may be good therapy. It's always good to know which way is up. Our adversities are most times building blocks. As the new framework is constructed, bitter memories fade.

You ask, "Who's under the hat?" That's the boy who never grew up until he reached his late sixties. He has a very successful brother and a flock of nieces he hasn't seen since their early childhood.

I look forward to your letters, Emma. A response to your latest will be in the mail over the weekend.

With Love,

Uncle Martin

In our excitement, letters couldn't help but back up on either end. In the one that he was about to read I told him about the two snowstorms and raging fever that hadn't stopped me from making trips to the cottage to scrape the blistered orange paint from the bathroom walls so I could apply a fresh coat of white. Where ashes had fallen from the wood-burning stove I had applied butcher's wax and buffed every floorboard by hand. Strips of wallpaper dunked in the bathtub and carried up the stairs now covered one of my bedroom walls. I wrote it all in great detail, then added that the process of transforming space was energizing me.

It was at this point in the letter that I revealed the secret fear I couldn't hold any longer. It was so unthinkable that I hadn't been able to say it to anyone out loud: I don't know if I'll be financially able to keep the school going into next fall.

January 16, 1983

Dear Emma,

Quite a picture you present of yourself painting and waxing through the flu and beyond. Yes, you are strong willed and have come through some hard times better for it. What parallels I am discovering in the makeup of two artists. We have our ups and downs, highs and lows, but we wade into the deeper water because we have the courage of our own convictions.

It pleases the old man that you have felt the inner strength from our correspondence. All may not be as inspiring as time goes on, but my hopes of this not being so remain high. Maybe, at this late date in my life, fate or destiny has brought about this relationship between a niece on her way up and an old uncle who has already beaten down the brambles and has found the ventures most interesting.

Let's hope your future dance school plans are not an IF, but if so, there will be greener pastures ahead. Hang in there. Thoughts of folding the school must not enter your head unless that is your desire. The stakes in lofty standards are high. Keep them! There is a market out there somewhere. You will find it.

Don't feel that you have to answer each time I write to you. You are a busy girl and there is little else I have to do. Until another discourse...

Love,
Uncle Martin

CHAPTER 15
The Nature Of Dreams

"Not bad," I told myself, in a sexier than normal voice, as I stood naked in front of my cheval mirror and patted my rock-hard upper thighs. I had taken to talking to myself a lot, in the past few years of living alone. The smallest bathing suit I had ever bought slid over my defined muscles without a tug or pull. My thirty-five-year-old mind had trudged through hard times, but my body wasn't showing any signs of it. I could smell the warm sunlight in the air. Dropping my head toward the floor I gathered up my hair and twisted the long locks around themselves, securing the knot with hairpins before grabbing my towel and running down the stairs. The lake was waiting.

I might have dashed right past the hidden activity if my cat hadn't been crouching in the doorway to the living room, white and orange fur shimmering as she wiggled in readinesss to pounce. Then I heard the delicate scratching coming from inside the freshly cleaned woodburning stove.

"You're done, Ambrosia," I lifted her out of her find-and-capture game and trotted back up the stairs, shoving her into the bedroom and closing the door behind her. My hands were eager to turn the stove's front latch and open the little metal door so I could take a peek at the contents: three baby birds that flapped, wings against wings, as they clung to the inside grate.

It was a delicate process, detaching the tiny fluttering orbs from their fearful grip, scooping them up, and carefully setting them in a paper grocery bag. Once outside, I scrunched another paper sack like a craft project nest and set it on the lower roof of my little cottage. Pushing aside the evergreen branches to tip the quaking bag, I deposited my cargo. Unharmed, and nearly fledged, they emerged in their moment of uncertainty. I was beginning to contemplate my own.

With each step toward the lake I attempted to push away a thought: *Nature isn't always kind to those who don't have the strength to move forward, those who aren't ready.* "Emma!" The familiar smile beamed from a porch up ahead.

"Hey, Peter." I tossed my beach towel over my shoulder and changed direction.

Peter J. Crowley had shown up at Evolution Dance six months before, looking for a job. I was formulating a creative strategy to market my dancers, and although there were no proceeds to warrant hiring him, Peter's portfolio of photographs inspired me. I agreed to a photo shoot.

After Giselle left the company, we had worked hard to regain balance. We were starting our second year without her. Other dancers had learned her parts and I was choreographing a new piece that highlighted my strongest dancers.

Peter's professional presence infused my strengthening dance company with hope. As we held our familiar poses to be captured on film, all of my dancers knew the emotional ride I was still recovering from, and we all felt ready to stand together and step out beyond our annual spring concerts. My vision of giving workshops in the public school systems that concluded with a performance was taking shape.

When Peter returned to the studio with his final photographs I was unshakably optimistic about my plan to catapult Evolution

Dance into the arms of our local community. I was comfortable enough with him to share my ideas about my new choreography, and I asked for his input. I told him then that my lease was almost up and that I had found a sweet little hideaway bungalow for rent at Congemond Lakes.

"Thanks for the tip." Peter offered a hug. "I love it here. I came up right after I saw you, and there was a rental sign. Where are you living?"

I turned to point out my corner hideaway, in amazement that he had landed so close. "It's great to see you, Peter. Our lecture demonstrations went well." I was leaning on the split rail fence. "I used one of your group shots with the press release. It landed on the front page." The day was too bright and promising to say anything more. I let myself feel the sun's warm rays and returned Peter's smile.

"Come for lunch tomorrow?" he offered. "I have some proofs I'd like your opinion on."

IN THE LATE MORNING PETER'S sunroom was shaded by an old knotted tree that hung over one side of his bungalow, the perfect muted lighting for assessment of his art. After lunch he poured us a second glass of wine and escorted me in.

We passed the black and white images between us; headless, legless, naked torsos, that called for consideration of each line and shape. In complete comfort we discussed the interesting play of shadows on smooth buttocks, breasts, and navels as if we were speaking of seascapes or succulent pieces of fruit.

"This is Renata," Peter announced proudly, running his index finger along the nipples of the tall model with ribs and pelvic bones protruding. "We've been dating for a while. I'm working with her later this afternoon." He went on to tell me about the series of blank note cards he was still in the process of choosing proofs for.

85

A series of dance shots he was planning to sell at a local card shop. "I love the pensive-looking photo I took of you on the floor of your dance studio, Emma. I like the contrast of the dark floor under your hand. You look as if you're in the process of creating a dance in your mind."

I relaxed into Peter's perception of me and shared the emerging thought. "If it weren't so introspective looking, I'd use that shot for my 'director's photo' in our next brochure."

"I'd like to use it in my series. With your permission."

"Really? Part of your card series?" I had to hear it again. In our impassioned sharing the soft footsteps that walked through the kitchen and stopped in the doorway went unnoticed.

"Oh," Peter chuckled, turning our attention to the husky dark-haired man behind us. "Emma, this is my housemate, Evan."

The wave of energy rippled from my neck to the small of my back when I turned and our eyes met. "Hello, Evan," I tipped my stemmed glass toward him and took my last sip. Peter was already closing his portfolio, clearing the cheese and crackers from the table, moving us into the kitchen. As I stood to join him I had to steady myself in the rush of that second glass of wine.

"The salad's nice and fresh," Peter lifted the wooden bowl to show Evan his culinary achievement. "Finish it up. It won't be good tomorrow."

I turned to the sink, the place I usually found myself during gatherings of every size and occasion. Running the warm water and rinsing away the leftovers grounded me in the present, protected me from the discomfort of unfamiliar situations. When I turned around, Peter had left the room. Evan was digging for the chopped vegetables at the bottom of the salad bowl.

"I'm meeting Renata," Peter reminded, as he returned with a jacket flung over his shoulder. I took a step back, toward the sink. "It was nice to see you, Emma."

"Yes, thanks for lunch."

With an abrupt goodbye Peter left me struggling with a wine buzz and the superficial conversation that was pushing me toward the front door, then onto the porch.

"I know a nice place for dinner." Evan took the chance before I completely backed down the stairs. "Would you be interested, later tonight?"

"Okay." I surprised myself. "What time?"

Is it okay? My mind questioned as I made my way back home. I was rerunning the last fifteen minutes like a movie critic looking for a bottom line review. *If Peter had any concerns he wouldn't have arranged our meeting,* my inner voice reassured.

I rested for a few hours, reapplied makeup to a fresh face, and pulled the embroidered cotton lycra shirt over my braless torso. I had grown to love my small breasts. I turned to admire my profile.

Over dinner the dancer in me sat tall, smiling and leaning into our conversations, but even a second vodka martini hadn't brought back the spine-tingling of our initial meeting. As inspired chatting poured over us from the adjacent bar, I once again retreated into my mind. *We have nothing in common.* "No, thanks." I held my hand up against the offer of dessert. "I'm done."

On our ride home my eyes closed to the occasional lights on the darkened road. Evan had run out of words. *A wasted night,* I told myself. The tiny lantern over my front door glowed in the distance, a beacon guiding me home. I thanked Evan for dinner, opening the way for my closing statement, but he passed my driveway and pulled into his own.

"There's something I want to share with you, Emma," he said, jumping out of the car and running around to open my door. I was already out. He had to be kidding. "I really think you'll be interested in this," he encouraged, walking confidently ahead of me. I didn't sense any risk in entering the dark house. Out of curiosity I followed him in.

He walked through the kitchen and through the open door to his bedroom. "Peter's staying at Renata's for the night." He tossed the words to me like a beach ball thrown with the anticipation of having it tossed back.

Unbelievable, I thought, leaning against his door jamb and examining the space. His cosmic bedspread looked like something from a teenager's room, a star-speckled indigo background covered in orange and yellow planets. *Not exactly a mood-setting accessory.*

My silence didn't seem to bother Evan as he opened a box of matches and lit the lavender candle that dripped over the edges of a rounded wine bottle. "Have you studied your dreams?" he asked, pressing the play button on his tape deck to add some ethereal music to the scene. He took a seat on the floor by his bed and was opening a dark walnut humidor. "Every morning after I wake up I purposely go back to sleep so I can participate in mine. Morning is the best time for lucid dreaming."

"Lucid dreaming?" I folded my arms across my chest.

"Yes. When I go back to sleep I actually reenter my dreams." Evan's stubby fingers had finished rolling a joint and he was licking the paper to press the outer edge down. "Because I know I'm dreaming, I can create them any way I choose."

I slowly slipped out of my sandals and took a few steps closer to Saturn. "Really?" I asked. "You create your dreams?"

"All the time."

"I remember a single recurring dream as a kid," I told him, sitting tentatively at the foot of the bed. "I jumped onto a pillow and flew down the stairs."

"You were astrally traveling," he replied without a second's pause. "You can fly anywhere you want, with anyone you wish. The journey you take is as real as any experience in waking life. You see, before you go to sleep, you can remind yourself to awaken within the dream."

"*If* I dreamed," I said.

"You do, every night. You just don't remember them."

I slid toward Evan, belly down, so I could look him in the eyes.

"Before you go to bed tonight, ask for a dream, Emma. Your simple intention will help you remember one – honestly. You should try it. Are you familiar with numerology?" He tapped me on the wrist and offered me the joint.

My defenses lay in a pool around me. This moment was too delicious to resist. With a deep inhalation I accepted the sweet smoke. "Numerology?" I barely released the word into an embarrassing bout of choking that I fought to clear. Evan's focus didn't waver as he removed the stub from my fingers and attached a feathered roach clip.

"Every letter carries a vibration." He drew a breath and held it in. "The combination of letters and numbers in our birth names and dates expresses the essence of who we are." He was slipping a different tape into the hinged plastic compartment.

This is where the martinis and marijuana took me out. The recorded male voice explained the vibrational meaning of "Evan Alan Brodin" as I slid off the comforter to sit beside my date. I stretched my long legs forward. My mind ceased all commentary. I focused on the pink polish that glistened on my toenails, then closed my eyes.

When Evan turned the tape over, I was too tired to go on. I thanked him for the mind-expanding evening and gave him an acknowledging hug. He stood in his own doorway and watched me as I slowly meandered back to my cottage.

I COULDN'T IMAGINE ANY PLANS for seeing Evan again. I didn't realize he was my initiatory guide, a messenger sent at the perfect time. My mind was too tightly wrapped around the fate of my dance school, the end that I had known, for a long time, was coming. My personal dream had become unsustainable, and I was mentally orchestrating the inevitable final performance of Evolution Dance.

This year no auditorium would be rented, no lighting set, no extensive choreography prepared. Our annual gala event would merely be a parents' night at the school comprising pieces from our lecture demonstrations. I hadn't made the formal announcement yet. I thought: *Everyone must know it's coming.*

Each morning by the lake, I mentally prepared to let go of the dream that had led me to construct a beautiful dance studio. The wood floor that Roger and Tony had built on a honeycomb footing was covered in state-of-the-art dance flooring. I had mounted thirty feet of mirrors on the blank walls. The school had not become a commercial business that sold "tacky" costumes and photographs to hundreds of kids. I provided stages, lighting, costumes, and free rehearsal space. I barely covered my rent payments, but my ethical commitment was clear. My students would never stand in front of a teacher who insulted them with phrases like "all those years of bad technique." My dancers were few, but they were strong. I created my school my way, and now all I could do was let it go.

"This is the final performance of Evolution Dance," I finally spoke the truth to the still faces that circled the studio. "I'll be closing its doors for the last time tonight. It's been a joy to work with all of you, and I hope to see you again in the world of dance. Thank you."

No applause lifted us up. No celebration or hugs. I hadn't invited family or friends to my awkward and flawed final presentation. The audience sat stunned. Silence carried each of us out into the darkness as my destiny came to be.

FOR THE NEXT WEEK, I woke every morning to face again the numbing heartbreak I had created. With no choreography or costumes to dream up, no music to find and consider, no classes to run to, I stepped into my bathing suit and mindlessly wandered toward the lake to sit and stare into the ever-changing sky. I waded into the water, floating on the surface, with no plans for the future, no stories of what had just happened, no conscious emotions.

Kathleen's picnic in her backyard with friends pulled me away from my solitary immersion. I knew that I needed some entertainment and interaction other than Ambrosia. A gentle breeze tempered the hotter-than-normal afternoon, so we could gather in the shade near the pool without feeling the need to jump in to cool off. As we sat over home-brewed iced tea, Analise made her way across the back lawn.

"Emma!" She waited until she was closer. "How have you been?"

"Hangin' in," I said. "It seems like it might be a good time to see you again."

"Yes, I'd be happy to make an appointment with you, but I'm wondering, with all the losses you've been through, have you seen a therapist?"

"I'm done with therapy, Analise." My volume rose. "I went that route. When I connected to my feelings and started to make some sense of things, the therapist pushed me out of her office. Her luncheon engagement was more important than me."

"I need to tell you, Emma," Analise spoke softly, "I don't believe in victims." I looked away. "We're not victims," she continued. "We're teachers and students for each other, here to learn our life lessons. I believe that every experience gives us an opportunity to choose how we want to respond."

I'm not a victim? My mind raged. *We're teachers for each other, learning lessons? Once these lessons have been ascertained... is that when we die?* My contemplation of possibly bringing death closer caused me to wonder if I might want to forget about learning these life lessons altogether.

"I have the name of a holistic counselor." Analise continued as I sat back on the picnic bench, resting my softening spine against the table and taking in a much-needed breath. "Maura lives near you. You'll like her."

The rainbow held my attention, splashed across the business card Analise offered. My eyes lingered over it before I slid the card into my pocket and returned to Analise's mysterious smile. She seemed to understand so much more than I was able to grasp. I surrendered my nod with complete trust.

MAURA SERVED UP MUGS OF hot herbal tea and kept my dramatic stories out of our conversations, focusing on the present: my feelings around closing the school.

"I try not to think about it," I told her. "All my pictures and newspaper clippings are in a box, stashed away in the closet."

"This has been a beautifully productive phase of your life, Emma. How do you feel about recording your accomplishments in a scrapbook?"

"I'd love to do that," I said in an almost-whisper as I lifted the warm mug of peppermint tea to my lips. I sent her a tender smile, drawn from hers. Maura was connecting me to myself in a way that let me feel the excitement of who I really was.

"What have you been dreaming?" she asked.

"I don't dream," came my blunt reply.

"Everyone dreams, Emma. You just don't remember them."

"This is so weird." A broad smile had broken through my astonishment. "Someone told me exactly that a few months ago."

"Well, that someone was right. When you begin to remember and document your dreams, you'll see what's going on behind the scenes, so to speak, in your unconscious. Your unconscious speaks to you every night in wild stories that may seem bizarre at first, but they can actually help you find resolution to your inner conflicts."

I was beginning to feel hopeful.

"I'd like you to pick up this book, *The Dream Game*, and a dream journal to start the process moving. Read a chapter or two each night and keep your notebook and pen by the bed," Maura prescribed. "When you wake up, write down anything you remember: a thought, a phrase – or even a feeling."

How much more simple could this assignment be? I agreed to her program, tucked my list into the pocket of my jean shorts, and headed for the bookstore.

MY NEW DREAM JOURNAL WAS as small as the paperback that sat beneath it. It didn't seem that a non-dreamer would need anything larger. As soon as the sun set, I headed for bed and sprinted through two chapters before marking down my intention: *I will remember my dreams so I can learn more about myself.* Ambrosia's gentle pounce on the bed startled me. I hadn't heard her come up the stairs. I extended my hand and she began to purr, signaling that it was time to place my journal and pen in the headboard cubby and turn out the lights.

Darkness still blanketed me when I rolled out of bed to make a trip to the bathroom. I had to force my eyes to stay open in order to safely walk down the stairs and through the kitchen. The brilliance of the throbbing fluorescent bathroom light startled my mind awake.

"Oh, my God," I said out loud, "I was dreaming!"

Promptly retracing my steps, I grabbed the little journal with one hand, pressing the other against the tiny opening that was ready to flow. When my naked flesh finally connected with the toilet seat, the surging simultaneous release of peeing and writing sent me into ecstasy. The writing stopped first, and I sat there, admiring a single sentence that stood out on the white page. It was as if I had just caught the biggest fish and reeled it into the boat without injuring a fin. Ambrosia tiptoed through the door, nuzzled up against my bare shin, then raised herself up on her back legs to run the side of her face along the the journal that lay open in my hands.

I closed the cover and turned out the bathroom light. Parading like the leader of a high-school band, baton held high with colored ribbons swirling through the air, I completed a pirouette and marched back up the stairs. Ambrosia watched from between the satin pillows as I reopened my journal in the first light of day to reread my entry:

7/29/83

> *People around me keep going faster and faster and I am trying to slow myself down.*

My single phrase was far from Evan's lucid journeys, but it had given me faith. Inner guidance was telling me the time had come to slow the frenetic surface reality of my life, which hadn't brought me any peace. I was oblivious to an understanding of the deeper implications of these few words, but the mere fact that I had willed them forward was an overwhelming reward.

Like an insistent child who knows what lies behind the cupboard door, I continued to open the dream gates every night. Waking to darkness, I scribbled everything I could remember in my journal before dropping into another dream. In the morning, I wrote more and circled every metaphor.

In one strange tale, I circled "the antique shop" and "the old record." I was feeling responsible for spilling a clear fluid onto a long-playing album and it had begun to melt. The process of dissolving my old recorded beliefs was indeed under way.

I dreamed I was trying to sing my own song but had lost the words. This was a revelation about finding my true voice.

When I faced Tony in a third dream, a baby fell through the cracks of the wooden floor. I quickly understood: *A newly forming part of myself was lost in that relationship. I am ready to retrieve and care for it.*

CHAPTER 16

Reunion

"Squeeze in closer," I directed, waving a hand toward Jonathan and Shari as I widened my camera lens. Kathleen pulled both of her children to her and Gina crouched down in front of the sign that read: *Yes, there really is a Kalamazoo.* An outgoing train rumbled as Peg ran up to meet us.

With baggage hanging from every arm, we chugged toward the parking lot, chirping like birds on a spring morning. Peg opened the back of her van and stepped aside, bubbling with plans for the upcoming week. As we bunched up around her she took another step to the right, staying in her own rhythm as she continued with the rest of her inventory: the sub sandwiches she had purchased at the church fair (hoping we'd all eat salami) and our well-thought-out sleeping arrangements. Peg tolerated the thrusting of suitcases into the diminishing space, but I began to feel angry. *Someone should take charge to make sure everyone has room to fit their bags,* my mind yammered as I set down my luggage and folded my arms, still steaming at Peg. Dad was always the one to pack the car. He made sure, from the beginning, that things were positioned in a way that used the space most efficiently. When he sized up each item and placed it securely in the back of our station wagon, I could feel his mind working, like it did before scribbling every word in his daily crossword puzzle. I turned to glare at Peg, for not being the one to take charge. *It's your car, for cryin' out loud.*

"We're gonna have great weather all week," she said and kept right on talking, as we arrived at the inevitable stalemate and began pulling out the closest items and repositioning them.

I huffed as I lifted my bag and pushed it as hard as I could, slamming the door shut. Peg opened her arms, dissolving my irritation in a second hug. "I can't believe you're all here."

"I can't wait to finally see your house!" Kathleen called from the backseat. Peg and Doug had moved into a large colonial that sat on over an acre of land. I remembered the pond at the back of the property, from pictures they had shared last Thanksgiving.

As the cousins rushed to reacquaint, the sisters "took the tour," slowly making our way back to the kitchen table. "I thought we could each choose one night to cook dinner," Peg suggested, "our specialty meal."

"I'm not sure the kids will eat tofu, Emma," Kathleen impishly interjected. She knew I had entered my vegetarian phase.

"How about alfalfa sprout burgers?" I tossed back with a smile.

"You'd better get out of my way when we reach the spare ribs," she rallied.

As we danced down the supermarket aisles, Gina threw caramel popcorn and two bags of candy into the cart, sparking another cackle from the group. In the comfort of our sisterhood, the natural rhythms of our interactions never skipped a beat. It seemed it had always been this way.

DAD AND MARGARET ARRIVED THE following afternoon, planning to stay only a few days, as part of a road trip my father had created around our reunion. Their house tour was barely completed, scotch-and-sodas freshly placed in their hands, when the white truck turned in to Peg's driveway and parked in the vacant spot. Shouts and enthusiastic nudges beckoned all twelve of us into the front yard.

A detailed leather boot with a long, pointed toe emerged from the cab; its solid stamp on the asphalt drive punctuating the hush of a dozen breaths held. One of our uncle's pale and wrinkled hands reached up to tug on the brim of his suede cowboy hat as Dad reached out toward his long-absent brother for the tender hug that would begin the needed mending.

The children hastily returned to their play. The kitchen bustled with activity. But I stayed close to the men whose opportunity had finally arrived. From a considerate distance, I positioned my camera to capture their mirrored ruddy faces and silver-white hair. I contemplated them as they spoke gently to each other, puffing on their cigars. Their identical laughter had survived over thirty years of separation. My mother would have delighted in those first hours of reunion. Was it possible that she could have helped create this meeting from the heavens?

On our second morning, while dew still shimmered on the grass, Uncle Martin sauntered along the perimeter of Peg's yard, a soothing melody rising from his saxophone. At the edge of the pond he paused, turned toward the back of the house, and began to play a new song. He had written in his letters about the gifts of music and creativity that came from his side of the family, but he had never mentioned playing the saxophone. I stood for a moment looking out from the kitchen, slid open the glass door, and stepped onto the deck. The Pied Piper's melody prodded and my bare feet danced across the lawn to meet him in a grande finale.

With one arm around his shoulder, I threw the other high over my head, thrusting my leg up and behind, bending it into an attitude arabesque. "Cheese," Peg called to us as she captured my most precious photograph.

After dinner, we circled the piano with arms interlaced. Tears ran from Uncle Martin's eyes as the three generations sang into the night.

In the following days I shared my bohemian life with my long-lost uncle; the moving from rooming house to rooming house during my early dancing days and my yearning for freedom, a passionate quest that we both shared. Athough he didn't go into details, he implied that he had been on some wildly dramatic adventures. He made no mention of the split that happened between him and my father, somewhere around the time that my parents got married. Whatever it was, it was behind them now. His little apartment in Sheridan, Wyoming, over a downtown bar, was all he needed; and of course, his old typewriter that continued to earn him extra cash and keep our connection strong.

"My dreams are helping me," I told him. "They contain messages that I'm learning to interpret."

"Once, I dreamed I was having passionate sex with The Madonna," he freely disclosed.

"*The* Madonna?" This dream was beyond my capacity for commentary.

On his final day, Uncle Martin returned to the sparkling truck he had rented for his excursion. He pulled out four signed and carefully packed acrylic paintings, splashed across cardboard backing and set into inexpensive black frames. "This is modern art," he explained, as if we had never heard the term. "The artwork creates itself." Proudly, he presented one to each of his four nieces.

We all promised to write as we exchanged our final hugs. He climbed into his white chariot and tugged on the brim of his hat one final time. *My camera*…No more pictures were to be taken, only a slow walk to the end of the drive, another visual to stuff into my bag of memories. As Uncle Martin took the next turn and disappeared from sight, my heart felt settled.

I HAD TWO THOUSAND DOLLARS in the bank, no job, and no prospects for one. Summer would soon disappear into the shorter and colder days, but I had no thoughts of it. Willingly, I gave up over half of my savings, dropped Ambrosia at Kathleen's, and headed out for a two-week dance workshop; a glorious playtime for souls like me, also searching for direction.

In the unusual September heat that followed me back home, I dropped my dance bag and groceries on the floor, pulled out a blueberry yogurt, peeled back the foil lid, and licked it. The back of my hand brushed across the mountain of mail, fanning it out in a physical display of all the responsibilities I had temporarily escaped. I tapped the play button on my answering machine.

"Emma!" The familiar voice shouted through the tiny speaker. "It's Valerie." *I haven't seen Valerie since I left the Dance Collective.* "You have to call me. My friend is opening a school in Worcester and he needs a modern-dance teacher. You'll be perfect for the job."

God, I thought, *how did Valerie find me? What's today? When do classes start?*

One thing became clear to me in that moment. In doing what I most loved to do, in letting go of trying to create the next phase of my life, the door had miraculously opened. When I made the return call, the teaching position was also still open.

CHAPTER 17

Relocation

Within two months I had found a rooming house and split my furniture storage between Kathleen's attic and Ken's garage. My ex-boyfriend had come in and out of my life between my move into the condo and my move into the cottage. He was ready to settle down, but I was feeling the winds of change beneath my extended wings, which were guiding me in a new direction. His love remained unwavering when I called and asked for assistance. He had a strong practical side. If I had wanted, Ken and I would have been fashioning a life together by now; the belongings I asked him to "hold for me" in his garage could have been integrated into the six rooms of his little ranch. Instead, he was arriving to help me move on with my life. I kept the antique chair with the carved lion's head I had pulled from our basement when Tony and I moved in together, and the expensive cheval mirror I had bought after our divorce. My coat rack, a functional tag-sale find, also made its way into Ken's truck before I said goodbye to my little cottage and turned to my next adventure.

I jammed my leotards, tights, and jeans into the drawers of the small dresser that came with my new room. Piles of tapes framed my boom box, poised in the corner. My pink and lavender satin pillows had endured another move. As resilient survivors, they stood proudly at the head of my single bed. With four other renters I shared one bathroom, a sitting area, and a paltry kitchen.

MY TEACHING SCHEDULE ALLOWED ME to sleep late every morning, which gave me time to enjoy leisurely entrance into my days. The peace of a midweek morning drew me to a solitary breakfast and a new journal that started with my latest dream:

FEAR OF GOING UNDER

I'm attempting to grow flowers by breaking them off their stems and sticking them into dirt-filled pots. I know I need to transplant them, but all the places I have planted before are gone.

I see a stick poking out of the dirt and think I can use it as a tool to dig. When I yank it free, I'm shocked. Instead of the thin stick, what I am holding in my hand is an ax.

I tumble into the hole I have created, water rushing in. I'm thrashing around to keep from going under. My arms clamp onto a large rock. It loosens and I have to let go. As it drops to the bottom, I'm floundering in fear; but finally, I pull myself to safety.

Going under. (I note on the left-hand page) Water rushing in: This is about an emotional issue.

The rocks: I need to let go.

THE AX: (bold letters, circled twice) sharp, cutting, dangerous, I don't know what to do with it.

At the time, I wasn't ready to see the ax as the unexpressed anger I might be holding, regarding the list of losses I had incurred, but I did find comfort in the dream's reassuring final revelation: Even though the mud almost swallowed me up, with persistence I dragged myself out.

HEFTY DRAMAS SURGED THROUGH MY first months in Worcester. The woman in the next room had just had an abortion. The woman in the room next door to her invited her rude, cigarette- smoking boyfriend to stay over on weekends. He got drunk, occasionally threw up in our community bathroom, and snored so loud I woke to the sound of it through most of every night he bunked in. These reminders of my dancing days in Springfield caused me to stay out most of the time, grabbing fast-food suppers rather than coming home to missing groceries. I was needing some moral support on the morning I called Kathleen. Jon answered the phone, eager to talk.

"I bumped into Angelo yesterday," he quickly reported. Angelo was Tony's older brother.

"Really?"

"Tony just became a father. Yesterday morning." Jon had also been the one to break the news of my ex-husband's remarriage. "It was a hard delivery, not like our kids."

"No." I said.

"Tony had to leave the two of them in the hospital for a few days."

"So he's alone?"

"Just for a few days, but everything's okay."

The baby I couldn't have is now his. My mind raced. *The younger wife has given him the ultimate prize. Now he has his own happy family, that son of a bitch!*

"Kathleen's out," Jon went on.

"Just tell her I called." I was speaking clearly, without a suggestion of the infuriation brewing behind my words. Slamming the receiver into its cradle and grabbing my keys, I flew into the bitter December air.

All day I wandered through the mall, trying on cocktail dresses, stiletto heels, the most revealing nightgowns. I mindlessly walked from department to department, oblivious to purpose or intention.

Picking up makeup, a candy bar – wanting, rejecting – until exhaustion dragged me home.

I dropped onto the couch and released one of my mother's forceful sighs. In the silence of the empty second floor, I uncorked the one purchase I had made, as I continued to chew on the piece of news like an old shoe dragged from a closet by the dog that has been left alone for too long.

I called Information with half the Merlot left in its bottle. Squinting at the unfamiliar number I had scribbled on a napkin, I jabbed my finger into each hole of the rotary dial, pushing harder with each thrust forward, forward, forward, forward.

"Hi Tony," I cheerfully dribbled into the phone.

"Emma?" he recognized my voice.

"Yeah, I just talked to Jon, and he saw your brother yesterday. I hear congratulations are in order," *for the goal I wanted, and tried for so long to obtain for myself.*

I sweetly continued on, as the good girl I had been taught to be, in the completely impulsive conversation that had no reason for happening, except that I needed some sort of release. How could I resolve the internal conflicts that Analise had pointed out through the double green lines in my astrological chart? Creativity and freedom? Or security and tradition?

I poured the rest of the wine down the sink and tossed out the empty bottle before feeling my way back down the stairs and out the door, to wander alone under the stars.

CHAPTER 18

Invitations And Unfathomable Truths

"Roomates Incorporated." The words jumped off the page, along with a phone number that led me to Joselyn, the cheerful, nonsmoking, pet-loving option I gratefully agreed to move in with. I could finally call Kathleen and let her know I had found a place for Ambrosia.

Another friend with another truck moved me into the old brick building with a wide staircase leading up to our second-floor apartment. Joselyn's silver-gray afghan met me at the door.

"This is Yasu," Joselyn introduced her expensive pet before escorting him off to her bedroom and securing him beind the heavy wooden door. "He'll be fine with Ambrosia," she said. "He's been around my mother's cats."

The floor-to-ceiling windows and wide white moldings made the spacious apartment feel like our old Georgian home. The size of it had sold me on the commitment. My new bedroom was almost twice as large as the one I had been renting, and this one was right next to the bathroom. Joselyn's contemporary furniture filled all the other rooms, and I wondered how she had managed to transport the glass-top dining room table without a chip or crack. With all my moves, I hadn't had a professional mover for one.

It was a few months into our lease when one morning, after staying the night at her boyfriend's, my reliable roomate announced her engagement. She kept up the apartment so her parents wouldn't know she'd moved in with her fiancé, leaving me to float in the large empty space until our lease came to an end. Ocean sounds drifted through the music that filled my bedroom as I lit candles and contemplated my most recent dreams. Beneath the thoughts of choreography and costume designs that kept my mind engaged, a natural internal rhythm was taking hold. With no distractions, I allowed myself to slide into the calmer cadence whenever I entered the sanctuary of the living space I was becoming accustomed to, and knew I would soon be leaving.

When the time came, Kathleen asked her son, Jonathan, to help me with my next move. He was a junior in high school and had grown so fast in the past year, I was still adjusting to it. I had taken a picture of him a few days before I moved from my little cottage. He was standing on the back of a pickup truck, beside his father and the nearly new refrigerator that Jon and Kathleen offered to purchase from me. On the day that picture was taken, my bed and boxes that had remained unopened for who knows how long were packed alongside of the refrigerator. Where my belongings were going, and if and when I would ever need or use them again, became a bit complicated as I approached my fourth move in two years.

I took the wheel of a U-Haul truck for this one, and drove to Kathleen's to pick up Jonathan, hoping all the furniture Ken had carefully covered in his garage for two years would fit into my two-room flat. I had signed my new lease without hesitation. It was one of the few places where I could take Ambrosia with me.

I dropped into a grounded stance and lifted one end of the television, then the kitchen table, couch, and loveseat. I took each well-placed step with Jonathan, up the stairs and into my new space, where, once again, I began to settle.

DANCE REMAINED MY FAMILIAR STABILIZING anchor, but there was no place within this dance community to extend my social connections. Living alone hadn't caused me to check out the bar scene, however. I enjoyed having my own space again, listening to the New Age tapes that were hitting the market, devoting more time to studying my dreams. I was okay with this space I now called home.

In the corner booth of my favorite restaurant, I took in the sun's radiance as it found its way through the leafy trees, playfully tiptoeing over my salad and a different kind of journal. I had begun keeping this little book between the front seats of my car, and often wrote in it when I took myself to the beach or treated myself to lunch at Natural Delights. Curious to know what was true on a deeper soul level, I had started the practice of asking questions about my life purpose and documenting the answers my mind brought forward. Today as I placed my pen to paper, the words came to me like a prayer:

> *Please guide me in my attempts to see the truth of my life. I don't choose to have everything fall apart from underneath me ever again. I'm ready to make the necessary changes. What do I need to know?*

This practice required a few moments of closing my eyes to outside activity in order to focus on my breath. Folding my hands on the open page, I allowed the first three words: "*Please guide me*" to permeate my internal gaze.

"You've gotta get a life."

My eyes sprang open. The attractive young woman who always waited on me was setting down a fresh cup of green tea.

"Thanks, Lori." I fumbled, refocusing my mind on her inviting smile.

"Have you been to the summer outdoor concerts?" she asked.

"I haven't been to a concert in so long I can't remember," I admitted, casually closing my journal on my unanswered question.

"Well, they're great, and this weekend starts off the series."

I folded my arms on the table and opened to the idea. I guess I believed I should "get a life." I had recently labled my new solitary phase as a "hermitage" in a conversation I had with a fellow teacher.

"We should meet at the concert and check it out," Lori pushed.

"Who's playing?"

I don't know, but they're always awesome, and it's just good to get out and be a part of what's happening."

"Yeah, it sounds like fun." I'd known Lori for a couple of months, and she seemed like a great friend to hang out with. "What time do they usually start?"

PEOPLE OF ALL DESCRIPTIONS, BEARING folding chairs and coolers, made their way between the idling cars in oddly formed bunches as the light turned red for a second time. I'd been driving around and around in search of a parking spot. My impatient fingers ran along the binding of my spiritual notebook as the light changed again, and horns honked. In a sliver of light between a mother and child, I saw a space open up ahead.

"Where have you been?" Lori squawked. I had run nearly all the way to our appointed meeting place. Engrossed in her perturbed huff, she simply turned and marched off with a "get out of my way" attitude. Blonde curls bounced to her bold cadence as the covered wicker basket swung in her hand.

Silky grass softened her steps, slowing her stride as she approached her chosen spot. Dropping a shoulder to release one end of the blanket she wore like a cape, she finally turned to face me and thoughtfully lifted the corners of one end with a shy smile. Reaching out, I pulled my corners tight and set them gently down before taking a seat beside her.

"This is lovely," I said, as she placed strawberries, cheeses, and a bottle of wine before us. I hadn't thought to bring anything.

Lori took her time pulling the tiny vase from her pocket, then a pink carnation from the basket. "Thanks to my neighbor," she confessed, dropping her eyelids coyly as she inserted the freshly picked flower. The crash of a cymbal startled me. I was caught pondering her preparations, speculating about her underlying allure, a charming appeal I hadn't consciously acknowledged. Depending upon the day, Lori's image ranged from strikingly pretty, to independently casual, to boyishly cute. In our most recent conversations she had mentioned other female friends in a way that implied what I couldn't be so direct about. Underneath it all, I felt perfectly safe.

With great care Lori sliced a plump strawberry down the center, releasing the succulent juices that dripped into my chardonnay. My eyes wouldn't leave her as she dropped one half into my plastic glass and, as if she had done this a thousand times before, slipped the other half into hers. She slid her fingers between her lips and very deliberately sucked them clean. Resting in the arms of darkness, I surrendered to the dampening ground.

When we closed the door of my apartment to the outside world, I fell into her. Lori directed me in the areas where I became reluctant, the passionate dance opening before us in an intoxicated flow, the first tasting of each other, as sweet as the berries we had just shared. Step by luscious step, we proceeded along a path I never could have imagined taking.

It felt natural to be in love with a woman. Intimately comfortable. Our unbridled attraction lured and carried us. With each morning I contemplated this new territory I was embracing. *How can this be happening?* When we were apart, I struggled to justify our blossoming relationship, but I was unable to concentrate on anything until she returned.

"We're soul mates," she said, wiping the glistening beads of lovemaking from the soft skin above my breasts. I believed this was true.

We established our place on flat rocks at the secluded hook of a meandering public beach, allowing the powerful incoming tide to engulf us. Naked and tan, to candlelit music, I rode on the surface of euphoria that pushed us effortlessly forward, with no awareness of the underlying baggage each of us carried and needed to unpack.

When Lori's guard dropped away, a timid sadness peeked through those hazel eyes, giving me a tiny unacknowledged glimpse of places we had come together to heal. Her excitement for walking on the physical edge continued to bring me out as my grounded passion pulled her in. Regardless of my constant inner questioning, I found the courage to commit to a relationship I couldn't even begin to understand.

I VISITED GINA, AND LOOSELY described my new relationship with Lori, but I hadn't mentioned it to my sisters who were busy with child-rearing and new jobs. I made the trip to Margaret and Dad's alone, looking forward to seeing Gina and Kathleen again.

"I haven't been with any of you since Christmas." I commented as I gracefully pulled my chair closer to the table and Margaret's rosemary chicken. As we dove into the cheesy popovers we shared recipes and asked questions about the Florida villa Dad and Margaret had the option to buy.

With so much to catch up on, Dad waited until coffee was served and the banana cream pie had been nearly devoured before announcing the news he had been carrying for almost a week. The heartbreaking piece of information hovered, like an avalanche suspended, until a silence in our conversation allowed it to break loose.

Some memories can only be recalled through a smokey-paned window. Uncle Martin's suicide is one of those. I remember Dad saying "Your Uncle Martin committed suicide last week," and after that, he seemed to ramble on, in his controlled confusion as he struggled to make sense of it. "The last year of his letters were crazy," Dad said, then he stepped from the room in an attempt to leave his emotions behind. My feelings froze over like a ten-thousand-year-old glacier.

Somehow, Gina knew the details: the sidewalk in front of the bar that stood underneath his apartment, the gun he always kept, and the early-morning hour he had chosen for taking his life. It all painted a brutal final picture of a complex uncle. His letters had become fewer as I moved from the rooming house to apartments, and his odd stick-figure drawings that preached about the perils of our deteriorating society had made me increasigly uncomfortable. In the past few years we had all pulled away.

Our animated conversation during our first phone call, and our discussions on the back deck of my sister's Michigan home, ran through my head as I searched for meaning in his tragic end, but I could find no solace and make no sense of such a shocking loss. *Only he could know why he took his own life,* my mind assured, pushing away any opposing thoughts and whispering the truth: *It's not my fault.*

As I sat in hope that his soul would be all right, the whole experience felt like a story from a book on my shelf. Uncle Martin was a fascinatingly influential character in the treasured novel, and our memories were the heartwarming chapters I had read years ago, and would forever hold in my heart.

CHAPTER 19
Answer To My Dreams

J ulie's invitation was the laying of a plank between ships, to rescue me from another sinking and carry me toward relief. After sweating through one of my adult modern-dance classes, she pulled me aside.

"A weekly meditation at my apartment," she explained, "with some friends."

I had completely forgotten the words of my very first dream: *People around me keep going faster and faster and I am trying to slow myself down.* I was unaware that our dreams notify us years ahead about the necessary steps that lie before us.

Steeped in the sweet smell of sandalwood, Julie's living room was illuminated by pillar candles. She had placed colorful pillows in a circle with crystals and an elaborate candlestick at the center. A piercing whistle quickly softened as Julie stepped into the kitchen and pulled the tea kettle from the burner. The conversation of the three women already seated around the table had remained undisturbed.

"Oh, here it is." A small-framed black woman with a tight afro and silver stars dangling from her ears turned a book toward us and lifted it up, with her finger placed at the beginning of a paragraph. "I have learnt from bitter experience the one supreme lesson: to conserve my anger, and as heat conserved is transmuted into energy, even so our anger controlled can be transmuted into a power which can move the world."

A collective "Ah" let her know Ghandi's words were being felt. From this contemplative place, we entered the circle.

We sat crosslegged on the cushions as we shared in "jai breathing," focused in the throat, sounding like the muffled rhythm of the ocean. With each breath I noticed I was moving closer to the calm that always sits at my center, the soft place my personality pushes down and covers with external distractions. I could feel the compassionate group energy widening until the room was filled with it.

My spine stood straight, and my knees comfortably touched the ground. The positioning of my upturned hands was perfect. But the energy between my heart and head was swirling. I kept swallowing to soothe the percolating sensations in my throat. My attention pushed to make it stop. Fingers wanted to clench. The urge to run away pounded inside my chest. Through tightly closed eyelids, I focused on the flickering light at the center of our circle.

No one ever remarked about my restlessness. This unconditional acceptance drew me back for more sessions. The resistance in my throat lessened, and our conversations expanded.

"Kripalu, Emma." Julie repeated the name of the the Ashram she frequently visited. "You owe yourself the experience. You'd love attending a spiritual retreat."

I carried her suggestion off to bed.

THE MAN BEHIND THE CURTAIN

I'm descending a beautiful wooden staircase bordered by walnut paneling. At the bottom I can see an old front door and a large window. The heavy drapes ripple, as if a draft has disturbed them, and I realize someone is standing behind them. A male presence.

I'm frozen in fear.

I open my mouth to scream. No sound. My heart pounds as I struggle to cry for help.

"Are you okay?" My eyes opened to Lori's concerned face directly over mine. "Emma, are you okay?" My mouth clamped shut. "Uh, uh, uh, uh, uh..." she pitifully mirrored back to me. Lori's spontaneous demonstration shifted into a relieved smile, sending us into a heap of laughter, but when I headed for the bathroom, I religiously carried my journal with me. *I need to know who the man is. Julie will help me with this.*

"I'LL BRING LUNCH," I ENTICED when I called to ask if she could arrange to meet me and give some feedback on my dream. She had dismissed one set of high-school students and was preparing the chalkboard for her next class when I rushed through her door.

"So... Emma, the man behind the curtain." Julie swept a hand across her emptied desk, symbolically making room for our mixed fare. "How we deal with the male part of ourselves," she explained, "the part that takes us out into the world, the assertive and aggressive part," she clarified, "is important to look at."

"I feel connected to my male part," I confidently replied, placing our sandwiches and napkins on her desk. "When I'm choreographing and teaching, I'm asserting myself."

"Yes," she agreed, in a wavering tone, as if she might be questioning my statement. "From a physical perspective, you have taken charge of things, but you might want to look at the emotional aspect. I was taught, as the 'good girl,' to be sure everyone else gets what they need, without any consideration of what *I* might want or need. But as I've grown into more mature relationships, I've had to take responsibility for myself by using more assertive actions, by actually telling people what I need in order to get my needs met. In your dream, you're unable to scream. Your voice has been silenced. If

117

it were my dream," she carefuly thought about her words, "I would want to look at what it is that frightens me about speaking in an aggressive way."

"I'll think about that." I shook a paperback from inside my folded sweater and looked to the clock. "I did pick up a book about numerology."

"I'm envious, Emma." Julie tapped her pencil on her list of numbers, rechecking her calculations. "In two places your numbers add up to 11, a Master number. Duplicate numbers indicate areas of one's life that will bring intense challenges and higher learning. I don't have any Master numbers in my configuration."

"You don't have enough challenges in your life, Julie?" We had to laugh. "I suppose you could change your name," I suggested.

She laughed again, but I wasn't joking. *Why can't we choose a name that creates a new energy, a new experience of ourselves?* "Oh, I almost forgot: I made my reservations for a spiritual retreat at Kripalu."

The bell reverberated through my announcement and Julie extended a parting remark. "Don't forget to take an Oracle with you."

"An Oracle?" My crinkled paper lunch bag missed the rim of the green tin bucket.

"Yes, the Tarot cards or Runes. Don't you have them?" Cacophonous chatter was bouncing off the cement walls, pulling us closer. "You need a set of Runes."

CHAPTER 20

Mind · Intuition

On my way to Kripalu I tilted my head toward the open window, allowing the fresh air to run through my long curls like my mother's gentle fingers. I breathed more deeply and attempted to quiet the mental chatter that had kept me company most of the drive. "We need to make room for our expanding ballet department," the notice had read. "Unfortunately, this will mean a cut-back in modern dance and jazz classes." *I won't be choreographing as much,* my mind confirmed, *but does cut-back really mean cut out? Will I be teaching at all? Do I want to start another dance schoool? Do I have the energy to start over?* My foot moved to the brake as I flicked my right signal.

"Let it go," I reminded myself, as I gripped the wheel and steered in a new direction. Lush green hills rose on either side of the wide entryway, and a lone visitor walked along the driveway that disappeared over a hill, then reappeared, leading me to higher ground where the students of yoga and meditation dwelled.

Packing had been easy for this weekend getaway. Leotards, tights, and a colorful sarong mingled with some basic toiletries. Of course, I had included the unopened box I had recently purchased at a New Age store that held a book of instructions and a small velvet bag of carved stones called Runes.

I lifted the strap of my dance bag higher onto my shoulder to the sound of clattering suitcases rolling in and out of the front doors. Confidently, I strolled along the tiled entryway to the front desk.

"Dorm room?" the cheery makeup-free woman asked, glowing with inner peace.

"Yes," I said, nodding eagerly.

"Down this corridor, to the left, past the gift shop," she directed after handing me a nametag and pointing toward the sun-filled lounge that had drawn some guests to the chairs that faced the silvery-gray lake. Everyone walked quietly, without gossipy discussions, many in solitude. Their self-focus seemed to connect them to an inner peace that shone on their faces. Simply walking in their presence I began to breathe more deeply. I felt ready to join in, but my thoughts took over. I began recalling the list of items the receptionist had offered up, like specials of the day: *dinner is at five, strip the beds when you leave, men and women eat and meditate on opposite sides of the dining room and meditation hall, the dorm room is on the right, across from the restrooms.*

God, check out the sandals, my mental engine roared at the unstylish Earth Shoes many were wearing.

Only upper bunks were still available. I chose the one in the corner, near the window, so I would wake to the first light of day. The simple sheet, pillow, and blanket folded neatly at the foot of the bed made me wonder, *How much do we really need?*

Maybe I'll check out the books in the gift shop, my curious mind added. *Maybe they're holding some guidance for me.* I climbed down from my freshly made bed and smiled at the woman who had just walked in. *It's time to explore.*

My return to the corridor slowed my steps. I noticed how easy it was to move away from the peaceful inner stillness. I silently reminded myself to pay more attention.

I wonder why the women and men are separated during meditations? The question popped in as I turned to view the life-sized portrait of the resident Guru, hanging outside the giftshop. His dark eyes stared into mine, as if he were offering the answer to my question, but when no answer came, I turned toward the rolling hills and headed for the brilliant green grasses that had sprung from weeks of April rains.

The doors to the dining hall had already been opened when I found my way to the two lines that had started to form; men on the left, women on the right. I exchanged a smile and nodded to another patient-waiter before I realized the discomfort growing inside me. We were gently moving along when the sounds intensified. Metal utensils, scraping the vegetarian drippings from stainless-steel pans, amplified an urge to turn and run. *Even meals without conversations?* I closed my eyes and tried to breathe my sudden anxiety away. *Someone talk about something!* I secretly begged, as diners tapped serving spoons against the metal containers to release clumps of brown rice from their curved surfaces. The tapping and scraping were waking an unconscious memory of sitting in my childhood kitchen where feelings of hopelessness filled the room, and I absorbed them like a sponge, to the sound of that same silent scraping.

My impatience forced me to rush through the organic selections as I felt the pressure building inside me. I pushed away the feelings that carried no conscious reasoning, my eyes darting across the steam tables as I attempted to fill my plate before anyone could pick up on my agitated "vibe." *If anyone notices, they're going to want to get far away from me,* I decided, rushing to the empty chair at the table that stood farthest away from my unacknowledged childhood reminders, forgetting a beverage. I retrieved one and returned to my table without taking a napkin. *I'm not going to reveal any more odd behavior by getting up again!*

When I finally gathered the courage to look into the faces that surrounded me, the stories I was telling myself were proved untrue.

No one was the least bit concerned about what Emma Morgan was doing in the line, at the beverage station, or at the back of the room. Some diners had placed their hands together in prayer, and many had closed their eyes. I set my fork down and rested my hands in my lap, eyes settling on the contrast of pickled beets against the shimmering greens. The unraveling had begun.

FOR THE REST OF THE evening I wandered, as an observer of others and myself. I sat and closed my eyes to the external activity, dropping into a more intimate place in search of my own inner peace. I hadn't realized how quiet the social areas had become. The ongoing video of the resident Guru had been put away, and I seemed to be the only one still roaming the halls. When I opened the dorm room door to retire for the night, the bright corridor lights sliced through the still darkness. I slipped inside and pressed the door closed. *There must be a customary curfew no one told me about,* my mind spit out dejectedly as I rummaged through my leather bag, feeling for pajamas and toothbrush. The unexplainable agitation resurfaced and clung to me when I returned from the bathroom, scuffed across the dark room, climbed into my bunk and fidgeted, hoping I was not disturbing the others. Minutes dragged into the next hour as I tried deep breathing. It seemed odd that outside my window the starry sky could feel so calm and protective, while inside my body it felt like tiny explosions were going off. *Observe yourself, Emma,* I remembered from our meditations; but like the swallowing that plagued me during those early days, I was efforting to make it stop.

When motion began to fill the shadowed room, it was clear that everyone got started very early here. "When in Rome," I remembered my mother saying as I followed the stragglers from the bathroom up the stairs to the meditation hall. Many carried pillows. Blankets trailed behind some, like a string of multiple Linus characters from the Peanuts cartoon. The previously announced line of demarcation between the men and the women was wide and well defined. The back rows were readjusting to allow space for late arrivals.

Our soothing meditation nearly muted my inner voice, but the rest of my day invited it back. I was now fully aware of my constant inner commentary and judgments. A midmorning dance class tranquilized it again, but my rambling resumed when I headed for another silent date with myself over lunch.

As I wandered toward the lake, I closed my eyes in the warm sun in an attempt to trust my downhill steps without the visual cues. The reddish hue inside my eyelids heightened my awareness of the fatigue I carried inside of me.

What can I do to release this? I asked. Then I sat and wrote: *Retreat. Observe. In time.*

At Julie's insistence, I had scheduled a bodywork session. The "polarity technique" sounded interesting. I liked the idea that it would put me back in balance by releasing energy from some areas and restoring it to others. On my way to the appointment, I began questioning whether I should have chosen a Swedish massage instead. At that exact moment, I came upon two women.

"I didn't know what a polarity session was," one complained to the other as they passed me in the hall. "I didn't feel a thing. I should have had a Swedish massage."

I almost laughed out loud at the immediate reflection of my doubts. My inner questioning had now become a private joke.

"We're always in the right place, Emma," I remembered Julie saying during one of our meetings,*"exactly where we need to be to learn what we need to learn."* I still required some self-talk to trust her words.

I lay face up on the massage table, fully clothed. The therapist's hands moved from my feet to my belly. The sadness that had been stalking me for nearly twenty-four hours welled up in my heart. My stomach began knotting. In the safety of her presence, my tears began to flow as I mentally replayed my marriage choice, my divorce, and the end of Evolution Dance. The deepest feelings that had no words surfaced, and the practitioner I would never see again truly heard the few statements I dared to reveal. As her warm hand rested over my heart, I knew this was a profound opening.

THE DORM ROOM WAS EMPTY when I returned to my sun-drenched upper bunk and placed the burgundy book of Rune descriptions in front of me. My fingers kneaded the velvet bag of small stones carved with ancient symbols. I slipped my hand into the pouch and carefully placed three in a row, from right to left.

The first marking was drawn as two triangles lying on their sides with their tips touching, like a bow tie. The stone, named *Dagaz,* spoke about my current situation and meant Breakthrough. *Yes,* I silently narrated, *I definitely just experienced some sort of breakthrough.* This Rune also assured transformation from the darkness that was behind me.

The second and central stone denoted the course of action I was being guided to take. Its symbol looked like a lightning bolt and represented Wholeness. In drawing this stone, I was required to become conscious of my true essence and bring it into form in a creative and unique way.

The final stone was to express a resolution. Two lines met in the shape of the tip of an arrow pointing toward the left. This stone was named Kano, the Rune of dispelling darkness and of opening. I reread one part of this message: "In relationship you may serve as a trigger or timekeeper to assist in a mutual opening up." *As I become more conscious,* I rephrased the words to better understand, *there is the potential to trigger a mutual opening in my relationship.*

I thought the stones were referring to my personal relationship with Lori, but like my dreams, the Oracle held more than one meaning. I knew on a spiritual level the mutual opening was about my deeper relationship to the Divine. To Source. To God.

I was in a trancelike state as I cleared my dinner dishes and headed outdoors again, making my way to a flat rock where I was warmed by the heat it had absorbed all day. The sun was melting into the far edge of the lake when I opened my journal and wrote:

Lead me where I need to go.
Gently illuminate my path.
Teach me to open without fear.
Reveal the parts of me that need to be healed.
Restore the voice that has been mute.
Soften my resistance until the rivers of enlightenment carry me home.
Amen

I finished by mentally acknowledging my growing trust in personal and intentional prayers like the one I just wrote. *I know they have the power to bring extraordinary answers and insights,* I affirmed, *if we can remain observant and open to any form in which they may come to us.*

I FELT LIGHTER WHEN I woke to my final day. Over breakfast there was no mental chatter. Comfortable in my body for the first time since I arrived, I headed for the bookstore to do some last-minute browsing. The empty elevator unexpectedly opened and, for no apparent reason, I stepped inside. It carried me to the top floor.

My first step into the empty corridor seemed to evoke her crying. Door to door I searched until I found the little girl clutching the hem of her nightgown in one hand, grasping the knob of an opened bedroom door with the other. Her auburn hair ballooned around her tiny face like a halo. Without a thought I scooped her into my arms.

"Mama," she cried.

"We'll find her," I crooned, as the rhythm of my steps softly rocked us. In her trembling she had discovered the knuckle of her index finger and inserted it into her mouth. "It's okay." I wiped the tears from her cherub cheeks. "We'll find your mama."

At the first sight of the woman, wrapped in a cotton robe and carrying a basket of toiletries, the child's legs started kicking. She pushed herself away from me to fly down the long hallway with arms open wide, her tiny feet scurrying until she could grab hold of her mother's cloth-covered legs. I quickly explained, the woman thanked me, and I returned to the elevator.

The downward thrust was like an internal shifting of gears that threw me into reverse. I was barely aware of the walk that returned me to the familiar flat rock, where I sat staring into a sky that was almost white. Waves of abandonment tossed me like a buoy in rough waters as I sat with my grief. I had never been able to feel what I was feeling now. *I will never again have the opportunity to wrap my arms around my mother or tell her I love her.*

Midmorning classes went on without me while I wandered back to my inner garden and looked over the bleeding hearts and forget-me-nots. Possibly I could pull out one more old weed before packing to go home.

With all my baggage loaded in the trunk, I headed east. Winding roads and scenery blurred into a collage of insights: *My busy mind is filled with endless storytelling. There is healing power in being present, allowing myself to be vulnerable and speaking the truth.* At the center of my discoveries I held the mental picture of the little child frantically searching for her mother, and I knew my own inner child was calling out to be held and healed.

"I got it!" I exclaimed aloud, smiling at my realization. "My waking experiences are as full of guidance as my nightly dreams. They're like *waking* dreams." My inflection underscored my excitement. "If I observe my life more carefully, I can understand even more about the deeper meaning of things."

As I balanced the steering wheel with my left elbow and twisted the cap from a bottle of spring water, I held a deeper understanding of the work I was being called upon to do: to heal the wounded parts of myself.

CHAPTER 21
Following The Heart

I had resisted the changes at the ballet school. My gnawing feelings about starting over were painful to face, but I could sense the need for change within myself, a longing for new direction. I had lost some of my passion for the hectic pace of pushing to create another performance. By the end of the school's conversion, I was actually welcoming the dropping away.

"It makes sense, doesn't it?" Julie asked when someone in our meditation group suggested The Holistic Center for Bodywork Therapies. "You understand how the body works, and what the muscles do. It seems like the perfect next step."

WITH SNOW SWIRLING OUTSIDE, LORI set out orange spice tea and hot strawberry turnovers she had carefully prepared to lure me from my massage studies. "A new recipe," she whispered through the half-closed door. "Better than anything I learned at the culinary school."

"They smell delicious." I breathed in, then released a heavy sigh, closing my anatomy book. I lifted both arms toward the ceiling, leaning back and releasing a huge yawn as Lori pushed the door open and waited. I could feel the heaviness around my eyes from trying to remember names of muscles and the locations of their attachments.

"There's a lot more to this than I realized," I admitted, following my partner back into the living room.

"You need a break," she said. She was already in the kitchen grabbing some napkins.

"I was thinking this morning, it's already feeling strange not to be dancing at all." I was leaning forward to inhale the pleasant aromas. "I love massage classes, it isn't that."

Lori chose the juiciest pastry with extra icing oozing down the sides, placed it on the red and white party napkin, and handed it to me.

"Bodywork is leading me to a more healing place," I admitted, "but I miss dancing. What if I've just let go of my greatest joy?"

I burst into tears. Lori pulled me to her and we swayed like willows in harmony with unsettling winds. I secretly felt I might die if I let go of such love for my life's work without having an equally passionate goal in mind.

"It'll be okay," she said. "You'll be okay."

As I SUBMERGED MYSELF IN my new studies, my fear receded. I knew I was destined to change professions. It was time to go deeper into myself and open to my sensitive nature. Massage classes offered more than a gentle relaxation of the muscles. I was learning about subtler connections through the human energy field. My hands already sensed energetic congestion: hot prickly sensations and cold stillness in people's bodies. As we entered a second semester of studies, our classroom discussions touched upon this energetic phenomenon.

"In any of these learned techniques, the simple act of placing your hands on someone can release barriers between you," our teacher assured in one of her moving lectures. "Swedish massage can offer an amazing exchange of energy and deep healing without any verbal communication. I strongly suggest working on family members."

I hadn't considered massaging my family, least of all my father, but for some unexplainable reason I was compelled to call him that very afternoon.

"I need practice hours for my massage class," I explained. "I'll bring the table, sheets, music... everything! It'll be like your own private spa."

MARGARET FUSSED OVER LAST-MINUTE PREPARATIONS. As soon as I arrived she began placing the chicken salad on beds of romaine lettuce. Excitedly I headed to their guest room to set up my massage table and tape deck.

"I'll take care of this," Margaret insisted when I stood to help with table clearing. "You can start with your father. I want to catch the beginning of the tennis match."

"That's my Margaret." Dad's prideful voice sailed across the table.

"Okay then," I said, "let's get started."

I led him into the room and turned from him to dig in my tote bag for the clock that would keep me on task. My hands remained warm as I grasped the plastic timekeeper, placed it on the corner of the bureau, and grounded myself in professional intention. "You can leave your underwear on, Dad, if that's more comfortable. You'll be fully draped. We'll start with you face-down, under the sheet, with your head in the face cradle. I'm going to step out of the room so you can get ready. Let me know when you're set."

Breathe, I automatically advised, sensing the soles of my feet on the rug as I stared into a smudge on the closed door; an unnoticed fingerprint Margaret wouldn't have allowed to remain if she'd seen it.

"Okay," Dad's muffled voice arose. "I'm ready."

He didn't say another word as I reopened the door, walked to the tapedeck, and pressed "play." Ocean waves joined in the delicate dance of a solo flute that soothed and settled us. With a few more steps I was at his side, folding back the crisp floral sheet, tucking it into his white elastic waistband, and moving it to the base of his sacrum.

I poured the almond-scented oil into my palm and rubbed both hands together. They were finding their rhythm, sensing the energy that grows with intention. They opened and touched down. Like the wind brushing the surface of a lake, our interface was delicate – the expanding rings rippling through his body, summoning a silent communication that released us from time. I could feel the space growing around us, where it felt safe to stand in our vulnerabilities.

I'm running my hands along the bare skin of my father, I acknowledged. Dry and leathery, it forgivingly stretched across his delicate bones. *I've judged his behavior for over half of my life.*

"Whenever you're ready, Dad," I whispered as I moved to the head of the table, "you can turn over."

His delayed response drew my attention closer. "Whenever you're ready," I repeated softly.

Rigidly my father turned to face me. The tightening around his closed eyes had created enough wrinkling that his tears had pooled around them. Wobbling between daughter and practitioner, I consciously rubbed my hands together again. The clear vision startled me, of my mother's hands as my own. With each stroke I could feel her with us, gliding gracefully down his chest and returning to his rounded shoulders. I knew he was remembering her touch.

Resting in the feelings, I opened to receive the unspoken gifts. I was grateful for the opportunity to connect without the congestion of words. We simply felt the love.

CHAPTER 22
Face Of Truth

As we set the clocks back, Dad and Margaret prepared to move forward, to their little villa in Florida. Before they left, he personally carried a small brown bag to Kathleen. The two of them sat over coffee and a conversation about the changing seasons and how he would miss them. Then she hugged him tightly and kissed him goodbye. With the little bag in hand, Kathleen climbed the front stairs and headed for the back bedroom to secure it in a private spot, under the halfslips in her dresser drawer, until the four sisters could gather again.

Peg's family of six flew in from Michigan for our July reunion. It had been over a year since we had seen them. The backyard erupted in joyful reconnections as we set up the potluck buffet, devoured our favorite selections, then cleared the remains from the picnic tables. Shari and Linette, the only female cousins, were chattering feverishly in the Adirondack chairs beside the blooming rock garden of their never-known grandmother. Lori floated in the above-ground pool, with Peg's sons splashing around her. Behind Jon's vegetable gardens, Jonathan and his uncles practiced their putting skills on an improvised "green," with an empty tuna can set into its center.

When Kathleen returned to the kitchen to check on the coffee and organize desserts, Gina and I eased off the wooden bench and walked toward the house without a word. Peg's red and yellow striped beach towel flapped at her side as she bounced across the lawn and picked up the jar of sun tea brewing on the deck.

"That goes back to the picnic table," Kathleen said, pointing to the tea, "and after we have dessert, if you want, we can go through Mom's jewelry."

"Mom!" Shari exclaimed, at the head of the line that raced in behind her. "You made your almond puff pastry."

Sweet delights were being lifted and transported, like buckets to a fire. Strawberry shortcake, a pineapple Jell-O mold, and a heaping platter of chocolate whoopie pies moved along the conveyer belt of hands as ice tumbled into a cluster of glasses.

"Let us know when you want to meet," Peg answered Kathleen, lifting the tea jar like the next item up for auction, before disappearing outside.

I stood on the deck and waved to Lori. She had found the badminton rackets, the birdie, and an eager partner. I smiled in gratitude that my family had been so unconditionally accepting of us, from the beginning; we had never formally "come out." Weeks into my new relationship, I traveled to upstate New York alone, to visit Gina at her apartment and tell her the news. When I announced that I was in love with a woman she was surprised, possibly shocked, at my choice, but never let on. I stayed overnight and my sister and I slept in the same bed. I think she felt a bit odd about it, but there was never another feeling of discomfort after that.

When Lori and I met, in 1985, living together before marriage had become accepted, but gay and lesbian relationships were still something most people didn't openly discuss. My parents seemed fine with my choice to move in with Tony; and to my family, Lori and I were a couple, just like all the others. I never received a word from them to the contrary. *My family is exceptional,* I realized, as I stood on the deck watching their interactions. *They have allowed me to become my truest self, without any judgment.* I continued standing on the deck, smiling about this for quite a while.

"One more year of college." I shook my head at Jonathan in disbelief as my words rolled into his conversation.

"I know, Aunt Emma, I can't believe it either." He wrapped his arms around me and kissed my cheek. "It seems like yesterday you picked me up in that U-Haul truck and we crammed your furniture into that little apartment. I was still a junior in high school then."

"Well, it's all happening too fast." I looked up to see Lori, holding a plate piled high with whipped cream. Peg was heading back to the house. "Sit here," I stood to offer my seat, tapping Lori on the shoulder. "We have to go through Mom's jewelry."

Single file, we marched up the narrow back staircase Kathleen had painted chocolate brown and stenciled with beige flowers. The tiny bathroom at the top of the stairs had been expanded and upgraded to enhance Kathleen and Jon's remodeled bedroom suite. Gina sat on the pillows at the head of the queen-size bed. I crossed my tanned legs, "Indian fashion," at the foot. Peg took her seat across from Kathleen, who was removing the bag from her bureau drawer.

"You know there are only a few things left to go through," Kathleen reminded us. We were more keenly aware of why.

When Dad moved all of his belongings into Margaret's vacant second-floor apartment, he couldn't easily return to the memories that sat above them like a silent tenant. He hadn't noticed right away. The men from next door, whom he trusted to help him move, had quickly moved themselves. With them went most of the valuable jewelry our mother had owned. When we met at Dad's for an unrelated occasion and he announced to us that our mother's valuables had been stolen, we simply accepted the fact. What more could be done? Heirlooms passed down from Nanny and special pieces given to our mother could never be reclaimed.

I recognized the tiny gold cross with the diamond chip on a tangled chain whose un-knotting had long been given up on. I remembered my mother wearing the gold starburst pin with its central amethyst. Kathleen set the two necklaces with matching earrings across from each other. The gold bow pin with four tiny rubies completed the circle.

"Dad had everything appraised," Kathleen explained as she unfolded a small piece of lined yellow paper and handed it to Gina.

"I'd like to choose by personal preference," Gina shrugged, handing the list to Peg.

"I've always loved her onyx necklace." Peg passed the paper to me. I slowly refolded it as the room grew still and Kathleen reached toward the center of the circle, to place the final piece: the cameo with the dented frame.

As my eyes lowered I could almost see eleven-year-old Kathleen, only a few feet in front of me, running from our parents' bedroom with her fist held high. At her heels I was reaching beyond my grasp. She had skipped around me and waved it in my face. I was determined to catch her. The bathroom door slammed.

The empty frame of the precious pin stood upright in the carpet, but no one moved to retrieve it as our mother's eyes filled with tears that slowly slid down her face. She was turning the dented, frameless cameo over and over in her hands, uttering her words without engaging her vocal cords. "I don't think it can be fixed." The silence drained us. "It can't be fixed."

"I'd like Linette to have her grandmother's cross." Peg broke my spell. "She's been wanting a cross."

I couldn't pull myself from the sadness that poured from the delicately carved profile of a woman whose eyes looked down and away. I felt my sisters' stares. "Yes, that's fine with me." I pointed to my choice. "I'm interested in the starburst pin."

"Would anyone like the cameo?" Kathleen finally asked.

"Not me." Peg's bluntness immediately freed her. "It looks too sad."

"I don't want it." Kathleen tossed in her own reply.

I held my eyes on the frame that courageously remained in integrity as it held the weight of our childhood years. *Someone's got to take responsibility,* my mind was demanding.

"I'll hold onto it," Gina ran in for the save, "if no one else wants to."

Our eyes met relieved smiles.

She lifted the joyless face to pack it away for safekeeping, and I nodded. Whether we acknowledged it or not, we were all aware of our mother's pain. In that moment, I tightly held on to a silent hope for a time when I could release my sadness around my precious, loving mother. *Maybe,* I wished, *when the time is right, her cameo pin will re-emerge to be proudly worn again.*

CHAPTER 23
Playing It Out

"Damn it, Lori, I don't agree. To my family that was rude." I turned from the sink and shook the vegetable peeler in her direction. "There was no reason to say that to my sister."

"Okay, Ed. Get on your soapbox and make everyone else wrong."

"I'm *not* my father!" The half-skinned potato flew out of my hand, barely missing her head and smashing against the kitchen wall. "And what you said to Peg was wrong."

I hadn't felt such rage since the night I'd skimmed my engagement ring under the washing machine. Only my strong conscience kept me from grabbing something heavier and trying again. *I will not allow inappropriate behavior,* my inner voice was screaming.

It seemed that one day a door had swung open and Lori and I entered this place of expressing ourselves, full throttle. We flared, apologized, and let things settle until something else ignited our fires. I turned my frustration on my peace lily, knocking it out of its pot and sending dirt into the deep recesses of the carpet. Where could I safely place the fury she could provoke in me? Repeated vacuuming and the focus on "getting it out" felt productive, but keeping busy only maintained my frustration.

"That's disrespectful," I'd scream.

"No, it's not," she'd retort.

We didn't even agree on what was "right" or "wrong." How could we find resolution? It didn't matter. I was approaching things in a different way, getting in touch with my true feelings. I was not going to hold my tongue, like my mother had, and kill myself doing it. No one was going to have that power over me. I was going to be heard.

In our battles to defend our beliefs, I wrecked a few household items and said some destructive things, but I decided it was worth it. By now, I had learned one very important thing: Regardless of the raw expression of my unearthed anger, Lori was not leaving me.

CHAPTER 24
The Book

In our weekly meditations, we didn't talk about our personal relationships. I hadn't spoken to anyone about my emerging challenges with Lori. No one had divulged any insights regarding their issues with parents or partners. The heart of our conversations held the details of the newest books on quantum physics, the healing potential of repeating affirmations, the energy contained in crystals and methods to keep them clear. We invited every technique into our discussions that would expel the nectar of deeper truths. We thirsted for it.

Tonight, Julie had expanded our scope of disclosure by telling us about a psychic reading she had recently treated herself to. "I'm telling you," she said, "when Samuel finished speaking, he asked if I had any further questions, and there wasn't one he hadn't already answered." Our eyes locked onto each other's in acknowledgment of her remarkable supernatural experience. "After telling me about a past life with my mother that, by the way, confirms why we still butt heads now, Samuel told me that my father's spirit was coming in. He was saying, 'Keep your chin up, Jules.' My father always said that to me!"

I lifted the little white tag that hung outside my steaming mug of orange spice tea and lowered the drenched bag a few more times, allowing the flavor to deepen as my mind wandered back to Howard, my intellectual high school friend from the Spiritualist Church, the musty den with clove-covered oranges, and the psychic medium's words, "You are holding your brother and turning the pages of a book."

"Emma, would you be interested in seeing him?" Julie asked, sliding the lemon bars from the other end of the counter. "I brought his phone number. Samuel Marks."

SAMUEL'S COTTAGE WAS TUCKED INTO the northern Massachusetts hills like a fairy-tale scene, with a sprawling garden and stepping-stone path that led to his planked front door.

"I'm Emma," I spilled before the door had fully opened to reveal a large man with mahogany eyes. I passed the folded paper, with the three questions I most wanted answered, from one hand to the other, as Samuel reached out for a strong handshake.

"Nice to meet you, Emma," he swept his arm in the direction of a room tucked into the back of the house, palm lifted in invitation. Eagerly, I lead us into his dark paneled office and took a seat on the leather couch.

His computer added the single modern touch to a room that took us back in time with pictures of Native Americans who sat around fires and stood beside horses and teepees. Diamonds sparkled on each side of his onyx pinky ring as he accepted the blank tape I had brought along. His broad fingers unwrapped the cellophane, dropped the cassette into his tape player, and attached a tiny microphone to his collar.

He must be credible, I thought, *if he's willing to tape our session. Maybe he'll be able to tell me if I'll return to dance. Maybe he'll pass on a message from a departed ancestor. Maybe he can enlighten me about my deeper purpose.* Questions about my relationship with Lori hadn't made the list that finally slipped from my fingers and fell to the couch beside me.

"Testing, testing," Samuel's deep voice startled me. As if no one were observing him, he went on with his preparations, pressing the "stop" button, then rewinding. When he cleared his throat, it sounded like the last productive cough of a long-standing cold, the final release that lets you know your body has cleared itself of any lingering congestion. His dark eyes gazed through my body and across the room, then returned to stare into mine.

"I work with Bernard," he explained, "a departed guide who brings information to me." I nodded as Samuel took in a few breaths, allowing his chair to casually twist to the left and right beneath him.

"There's a Native American woman standing behind you." He was looking through me again. "In a white rawhide dress. Do you recognize her?"

From the time I began practicing energy balancing protocols, I had sensed her at my side but hadn't told anyone. "Yes, I recognize her."

"She's a spirit guide who works with you, Emma. She carries a basket of healing herbs."

"Yes, I've seen it."

"This spirit woman assists you in healing sessions." He paused for a moment, focusing far away, then looking into my eyes again. "What do you do for a living?"

A psychic reader shouldn't have to ask me for personal information, I judged, but offered up the answer anyway. "I'm studying to be a massage therapist."

"Yes, this is good. This is where you are meant to be." I sat taller and folded my hands in my lap, waiting patiently for his next words as he squinted and looked over my right shoulder. "I see her, Bernard," his voice raised. "Your mother is here," he announced, in a softened disposition. "Has she passed?"

"Yes, about ten years ago."

"Well, she's here. And wants you to know that she's at your side whenever you need her. She's telling me that she wants to help you. You only need to ask for her help." He was squinting again. "You also have an uncle that's coming through from the other side."

"Uncle Martin?"

"Yes. He wants you to know he's okay."

My sigh carried in it the unspeakable, and all the unspoken feelings.

"He was ill, you know. He didn't want anyone to know it, but your uncle was very ill."

I closed my eyes, to allow myself to absorb his words.

"He was confused for a while upon his departure, Emma, because his exit was so abrupt. But he's telling you that he's okay. Just a moment, Bernard." Samuel's spiritual connection seemed to be undergoing some negotiation.

"Yes, I see them. Yes, I know. Now Emma," he was inspecting my energy field again, psychically viewing the space around its outer edges, "there are stars. All over. All around you. I've never seen anything like this. Stars as big as your hands. The area around you is filled with light."

"I'm using my hands in a new way," I felt free to disclose. "I'm studying energy work at the massage school."

"Stay with it. This is your calling."

The room grew still as he returned to the scanning mode of a sonar device, listening with a deeper sense most of us are unaware of, like a dog listening for the high-pitched whistle only he can hear.

I was startled by the immediate change in Samuel's energy. He slumped in his chair and opened his mouth in one slow yawn that initiated another. He intentionally inhaled, as if the breath held a meaning he could sense and accurately respond to.

"You're tired, Emma." He spoke slowly. "I feel in this time period you are emotionally very tired." Another yawn. "You are typing on a typewriter or a computer. Oh yes... you're writing a book."

"A book?" My forehead scrunched in an exaggerated expression.

"You have something important to share with the world." Samuel ignored my dramatic bewilderment. "You're going to write about it. You'll publish information that will help people understand something better." He paused again.

"Me, a writer?"

"Have you been writing?" he asked.

"Well..." *Should I tell him?* "I do have a steno pad in the car. Occasionally I jot down questions. And prayers. Short thoughts."

"I mean automatic writing. Have you been doing any automatic writing?"

"Well, I've been writing in a different way. Sometimes without even thinking. It sort of writes itself. When I reread it the words don't always sound like mine."

"Do you have it with you?"

"Yes, in the car."

"Let me see it at the end of our session. You need to continue this writing. It's an important avenue for you. I'll give you an affirmation to help with your energy, to rejuvenate you when you sleep." Samuel dropped into another long pause. "Mmm... your father's having mini-strokes. He's not aware of them yet. He's not close to transition now, but he is moving toward it in this way. These strokes will affect his memory and communications with you in a while. Do you have any more questions?"

As Julie had predicted, Samuel had more than answered every one. Before I slid back behind the steering wheel, he affirmed my writing. With a new appreciation, I returned my journal to its practical place, between the front seats.

Stars, as big as my hands, I contemplated, as I made my way home. *Why will I be so tired, I wonder, in the timeframe he demonstrated so clearly? And what's the deal with this book?*

CHAPTER 25
The Body and Emotions

"Often our students move out of unhealthy jobs or relationships during their studies here," the director of admissions had shared on our first day of orientation. "Because bodywork supports our core healing and facilitates energetic movement, doors frequently open to significant change."

Articles and books were falling into my hands, describing techniques designed to release negative emotions implanted in our body during traumatic times. I was learning that our muscles and our fascia (the thin layer of tissue that encases the muscles) hold cellular memories of every life experience. I rushed to explain this amazing phenomenon to anyone who would listen.

"You would love rebirthing," Naomi suggested as she finished practicing on me. We had been in every class together since my first day at the holistic center, and we had become close friends. Naomi knew how enthusiastic I was about the energy-based therapies that connect the body-mind in a subtler way than Swedish massage. "Rebirthing is a technique that puts us in touch with our unconscious blocks, and helps to release them. Graham is a psychotherapist I've known for a long time. He just finished his training."

GRAHAM HAD AN IN-HOME OFFICE at the end of a long, winding road, lined with well-cared-for homes. I had left plenty of time, so I slowed to observe the gardeners who were stooped over their flower beds, pulling out remnants of the past summer, making way for new growth. His old screen door hung loosely on its hinges. It looked as if one more opening would knock it off like a dead blossom and send it across the front porch, but it held when the tall, bearded man swung it open to greet me.

"Emma!" Something delicious was simmering on the stove. "I'm Graham." His committed handshake pulled me into an entryway that was permeated with the aromas of basil and oregano. "We'll be working across the hall," he pointed to the converted den. "Make yourself comfortable. I just need to turn off the soup."

I slid out of my sandals and dropped onto the soft floor mat at the center of the room, crossed my legs, and adjusted my position until I began to feel myself settling in. "You'll be lying down," Graham explained, as he returned with a pillow to place under my knees. "Now, I'm simply going to ask you to breathe in and out without forcing your breath." His deep voice was soothing. "Do you need something under your head?" He was handing me another pillow. "This is a continual breathing pattern," he went on, as I stretched out, closed my eyes, and rested the back of my hands beside me on the mat. "In and out." Graham was slowing his words. "Without stopping in between."

"Okay," I agreed, "but I have to tell you, Graham," my eyes sprang open, " I don't understand. You just want me to breathe?"

"I just want you to breathe," he echoed. "This work has helped me immeasurably with my own process, Emma. If you feel comfortable just try it with me. Breathe in and out. Don't stop in between."

The sound of my breath, being pulled into my expanding lungs and then being released, grounded me in the present moment, where I observed the length of each inhalation, and I focused on not holding my breath, immediately releasing into the exhalation. I became a little self-conscious, then my mind took over.

"Focus on your breath, Emma." Graham seemed to know I was thinking. Patiently, he sustained his mantra as I struggled with my objections, but my breath did keep returning a wandering mind to the present moment. I became less aware of the fact that I was lying on a mat on the floor, and found my awareness was going deeper inside of myself. The energy around me felt lighter, as if it were thinning out. I felt more and more a part of that energy as Graham continued his coaching. "Deepen your breath. Let yourself go." My physical being seemed to dissolve into a weightlessness astronauts must feel when gravity no longer holds them down. The breath had freed me from physical boundaries. I actually seemed to be expanding, like a bread dough tripling in size from the activated yeast.

I don't know how long I hung out in this uncharted space before becoming aware of the heaviness in my chest and difficulty in taking a deep breath. A numbness made me feel disconnected from my legs and I felt an internal pressure pushing upward, into my throat. I felt it for a while. From behind fluttering eyes I was witnessing, with an emotionless fascination. I felt completely connected to my essence, my soul. Secretly I wondered if I could make the choice to break free of my physical form. As I observed from this pain-free place, I was fearlessly considering continuing the journey and forgetting about returning. It was as if I remembered taking this familiar path from the physical before... possibly, at the end of many lifetimes.

In the midst of these insights, my breath had become shallow, and Graham had changed his breathing mantra to affirmations. "You are safe. You're at peace. You are free."

I suddenly became aware of my body, lying on the floor, as straight as a board. I couldn't feel any sensations in it, except around my upper chest and head. I felt I was locked in position, like a mannequin. Concern pried its way in. I knew it was time to come back. When I calmly opened my mouth, I could barely speak. "My hips and legs are numb," I told Graham, through pursed lips.

Almost immediately, an ecstatic release through the lower half of my body freed my legs and feet. My upper body remained in tetany, a temporary state of paralysis I would learn more about when this session came to a close. I slowly peeled my eyes open and, in utter fascination, stared at my arms. They were sticking straight out from my sides, and my hands were locked in a fully flexed position.

"Concentrate on your breathing, Emma." Graham's voice became stern. "This is important. We need to deal with this issue for your arms to relax."

What issue?

Do you want to hit your father?"

My father? I searched my mind for an answer.

"Do you want to tell him how you feel?"

Any conversation we had shared during this journey out of my body had completely vanished, like a dream lost upon awakening.

"No. I don't have anything to say to my father."

Graham's words focused me. "Bring your attention into your body, Emma. To the sounds in the room. To your fingers and hands." I was regaining stability. Graham left the room and returned with a glass of water. I sat up with arms trembling, and took a sip.

My next half hour was spent integrating the physical effects of my profound experience. Whatever issue I was dealing with concerning my father had consciously come and gone like a flash, and now, I felt shaky as Graham insisted on walking with me to a pond close-by.

"Our inner process isn't logical or predictable," he first clarified. "Rebirthing is a spiritual cleansing process, a way to connect us to the Divine energy source." He took my arm and guided me down a pebbled path. "It rarely happens, but when it does, tetany indicates a fear that stops the flow. Your breath became shallow at that point.

You may have subconsciously touched upon a deep trauma, possibly from as far back as the time of your birth."

I breathed in the dimming sunlight, pulled off my sandals, and splashed my toes in the cool water. "It felt so odd," I told him, "having my muscles actually tighten like that."

"Well, it probably won't happen like that again," he reassured. "If you'd like, we can make another appointment in a few weeks."

I did agree to another appointment with Graham, and he was right, it didn't bring up the reaction of my first session. On that initial night, when Graham had said good-bye, I sat in the car with an occasional internal chill still running through me. I understood, from energy sessions I had received before, that his intermittent shuddering was indicative of a release of core energy, and although I didn't understand all of what was going on, I was grateful for the opportunity to release it. My attention shifted to my leg muscles, which were pulsing as if I had undergone an intense physical workout.

Held in an isotonic position for such a long time, they would certainly feel this way, I told myself, but I was more intrigued with how my body had responded in such a physical way to emotions regarding my father. Unresolved issues had definitely taken up residence in every cell of my body.

CHAPTER 26

Sedona

"I love the energy in Sedona!" Naomi's excitement surged through the phone lines. My massage-school friend had returned three times to the renowned region of prominent "power spots," vortexes I was voraciously reading about. The opportunity to join her and a couple of her friends for a week-long stay at the mystical destination felt like a call from beyond, a proposal of union with the unseen higher forces that abound in Sedona's red rocks. I was quick to say yes, and Naomi insisted I call to schedule an appointment with her new friend, Alan Hart, for a past-life regression on the final day of our retreat.

Lori had been to Phoenix, had no interest in taking another trip to Arizona, and wasn't the least bit curious about the intriguing characteristics of the energy vortexes I couldn't learn enough about. Regardless of all that, she contested my traveling without her so early in our relationship. But as I packed and continued to plan, she realized that she wasn't going to keep me from going, and she reluctantly gave up the fight.

"This entire area has amplified energy," Naomi explained on our way from the airport to our motel. "It's not only the familiar power spots like Cathedral Rock and Boynton Canyon that carry this energy. I don't know if you've read about this, Emma, but I know it to be true: Because of Sedona's energy vortexes, experiences you can learn from will come to you, here. Unresolved issues will come up, right in your face."

This was quite a thought to consider, that simply being in a location with a certain energy could draw experiences to you that could help you grow spiritually.

"Cool," I said, smiling with the others as we continued driving upward into the Sedona hills.

Before my friend was done checking us in, I slid the motel key off the counter, impatiently waving it in the air as I headed toward our room. My stomach growled as I rolled my suitcase up to the door. *It's past dinnertime in Massachusets*, my mind reminded me as I fumbled with the key, attached to a purple tag with the number 5 clearly stamped at its center. I turned it over and attempted to insert it again.

Naomi was halfway to our room when I passed her, walking in the opposite direction with my head lowered. "Emma, where are you going?"

"It doesn't fit." I waved the key at her again.

The comment she had made on the drive from the airport, about how deeper issues come up in your face in this Sedona energy, didn't immediately come to mind as I stomped back to the office to exchange keys. I wasn't ready to let a little incident of getting locked out become a personal issue of being resistant to opening to this new experience. A Mexican restaurant was waiting, and a trip to Airport Mesa for an impeccable view of the constellations. Add a good night's sleep to all of that and I nearly forgot the "insignificant" key episode. When we all met at the rented car to head out for breakfast, I extended an open hand, with an offer to drive.

We toasted to Naomi's fourth visit, sipping freshly squeezed orange juice as we acknowledged new friendships and visions of adventures ahead. "This is why I want to move here," our host sang into the air, raising her chin as high as she could, looking almost backward to convey her heart-opening experience, "the open skies that go on forever."

Drenched in our grounded connections to each other and this new energy, the four of us spread out as we wandered back to the car, open to any spiritual messages we might see in the clouds or hear in the next gentle wind. I was digging in my purse for the keys.

"You might want to check the ignition," someone calmly suggested. My eyes lifted to the embarrassing lockout.

"I'll inquire at the restaurant for a coat hanger," another voice offered.

Like a moving meditation, the group assisted in unwinding the metal wire and verbally guiding the newly created tool through the tiny opening at the top of the window and around the plastic lock. One gentle tug and we were on our way, but my mind was now running in circles like a rebellious mutt whose leash has been unexpectedly let go. *How could I have been so stupid? Why do I keep getting locked out?*

The judgments hounded me all the way to Naomi's favorite New Age shop, where ethereal music flooded every room. I walked past the incense burners, heading for a quiet corner in a back room that held rows of appealing book titles and shelves of amethyst, rose quartz, and clusters of crystals.

I came to a large framed print of a starscape and I knelt on the soft carpet to stare into it. *Where must I look?* I asked the painted heavens for healing advice, sitting still and opening to the energy around me. I was waiting for a sign.

The musical selection changed. *The sign?* And then I saw it, a purple bag that must hold an answer. I stood to reach for it.

Bang! My forehead smashed into the overhanging shelf, nearly sending me back to my knees.

"God," I cried out in the quietest whisper, holding my hand over my right temple, hoping no one had seen. *What is going on?*

When we returned to the motel, a phone message was waiting for me. Alan Hart had been called out of town for the next week. He was canceling our past-life regression appointment. *Okay,* I began to line up the prominent experiences of the last twenty-four hours: *First, I'm given the wrong key to our room, then I lock everybody out of the car, then I ask for guidance and I get clobbered on the head. I come home to the message that Alan Hart is leaving town, so the one thing I chose to experience while I'm here isn't going to happen. What the hell is going on?*

In a smoldering funk, I sat in front of the television, turned it off, and disappeared into the bathroom, where I pulled my hair into two coarse pigtails that stuck out in uncontrollable spikes. When I came out, I pried open a box of cheese crackers and chomped away at my disappointment.

"What's going on with your hair?" Naomi asked playfully.

"It isn't funny," my voice snapped. "This dry weather has taken out all the curl. I don't know what to do with it. I hardly recognize myself." Hands that wanted to fist tore out the elastic bands and dug through my makeup bag for a resolution. Two tortoiseshell combs gave my shapeless hairstyle a second chance.

"I'm going to a healing circle tonight." Naomi leaned forward, looking at my sad face with an amused grin, "if you'd like to come."

"I think I need it. And a swim, if I have time. When are we going to dinner?"

"Not for another couple of hours, Emma. You have time."

My feet shuffled off toward the pool, all the way to the end of the parking lot, where the blue-tiled oasis stood unused. No distractions from my predicament waited for me here. I slipped into the warm water and invited the sunlight to penetrate my bruised forehead.

My pink toenails broke the water's surface as I opened into a restful float.

"I give up," I said to the clear sky. "I willingly release the resistance that's keeping me locked out and trying to get my attention." I tried to be clear by using the metaphoric images of my recent experiences. I turned them into a positive affirmation: "I am open to receive what I'm here to learn." Taking a deep breath, I returned to my solitary float, in complete acceptance of this journey of locked doors, missed meetings, and energy vortexes.

CHAIRS AND PILLOWS WERE BEING placed and moved as the meditation group created its own formation. I found my spot directly across the room from Naomi, who hugged a short man with curly silver hair and a manicured beard. I closed my eyes and went inward, feeling happy for her, happy that she had found her spiritual family here. I held the intention of finding my own inner peace, in whatever way I needed. As the group grew larger I continued to hear the shuffling of pillows and the moist skin of warm bare feet sticking to the wood floor as the other guests walked from one spot to another.

I heard the sound of a heavy, uneven gait that came close to me and had stopped. My curiosity caused me to open my eyes to the short gray-haired man who had been talking to Naomi on the other side of the room. "Emma?" he asked, "I'm Alan Hart. My plans have changed."

BOYNTON CANYON WAS THE ONE place Naomi wouldn't leave Sedona without visiting. It was our final morning and she assured me we had plenty of time to savor the experience and still be back before my two o'clock appointment with Alan.

"It's an unmarked lot," she said, in an effort to help me find the hidden plot of sand where she always parked. "There!" She pointed as we bounced through the dusty entry and she pressed down on the brake.

"This is the most difficult way in," she explained, as the ignition dropped silent and I threw the strap of my camera over my shoulder. "The last time I was here, I drove around to the other side." She pointed off into the distance. "They're building a huge hotel over there. Since they've bought the land and made it private property, the Native American elders can't get in to perform their sacred rituals anymore. This side is too steep for them to climb.

"This is their land," I cawed in disbelief. "In this consciousness-raising place the elders can't get onto their land? Who makes these decisions?"

Naomi locked the car and lifted her shoulders in question.

"So they can't come here anymore?"

"No." We stopped talking, breathed into the red rocks, and opened our hearts to the reality together. "I guess, not on their own. I'll meet you back here in an hour."

NAOMI DISAPPEARED ON A PATH she seemed to know well, as my eyes drifted in another direction, toward an unfamiliar chirping at the crest of the hill. I could barely distinguish the physical form of a tiny bird, half-hidden in the thicket up ahead. In a rush of unexplainable feelings, my breath weakened. Tears filled my eyes. I felt as if I was returning to a precious place I had intimately known long ago.

The majestic wall of red rock that cast its shadow into the chasm seemed to have been carved by master craftsmen. Every chiseled corner seemed perfectly placed. Each of my steps drew me deeper into the energy of it, into the timeless place I had experienced in meditation classes and on Graham's rebirthing mat. The tiny bird disappeared over the hill, but I found her again when I reached the top. Standing so close to the breathtaking formations brought me to my knees, intensifying the sensation of boundarylessness.

Rattlesnakes. A warning from the guidebook found its way in. *A water bottle.* I hadn't brought one along. Fear of the snake felt more pressing as I knelt on the flat rocks these snakes were said to enjoy sunning themselves on. *There's no one to help if I'm bitten.* A moment of sacred trust invited me to place my tired hands on the rocks' warmth. The earth seemed to pulsate, lifting my right hand and then the left in synchronized undulating movements, like a calm surface of the ocean. I felt the brick color circulating through me as I was lifted into a swirling surrender.

When I stood, my feet took over. No thoughts arose to change my uncharted course. I stepped off the edge of the path and down a steep slope of crushed stone, toward the valley below, eyes unfocused. The sun, rocks, and brush around me felt alive, like animals are alive. My palms pulsed with their life force as I reached the bottom and headed off to the right, deeper into the red.

I don't know how long I had been walking when the sight of it sent me reeling into a gaping hole. The broken integrity of the energetic vortex sent humbling shivers through me. Dismantled clusters of rock hung precariously over mounds of pillage. The bulldozers sat half hidden in the distance, submerged in another section they had scraped open. Overwhelming feelings returned me to the cavity I had lost myself in. I could hear the earth crying.

"What can I do to help?"

Witness, was the reply.

The colorful little stone that caught my eye was unlike any I had seen in this red-rock world, with a blue-green tint and rounded beige surface. I picked it up and rotated it in my hand to get a better look. The two fangs were still intact. I was holding a perfectly preserved snake skull. Peering into the roof of its mouth, I could see through the holes that once held its eyes. Beneath my pounding heart, I was aware of the synchronicity of the snake energy that had frightened me at the outset. Suddenly I became aware of the time. *The time? What time is it?*

Our designated hour and another ten minutes had passed. I had completely lost my bearings. Looking back to the tiny snake skull in my hand, I remembered. *One should never take anything from a sacred site.*

I set my treasure on a jagged ledge, giving thanks for the great gifts I would later integrate, and turned toward a path up ahead. With no idea where it led, I walked at a swift pace.

Between thoughts of how I might find my way out, I began to feel the oppressive heat. *No water bottle,* I reminded myself. The towering red rocks to my right let me know I was far from the road where we had parked the car. The way out was again to my right, a steep, overgrown, pathless ascent. With my heart racing, I rushed forward, the skull and its message haunting me: *Slip out of your old skin and leave it behind.*

I lept over something that slid beneath me. *It couldn't have been a rattlesnake.* As swiftly as a lightning bolt, it had slithered across my path, and my feet now pounded the dusty ground to get as far away as possible. Every stick and broken branch called my attention as my breath shortened in the thickening air. My accelerated heartbeat filled my ears and my throat tightened as I forced myself to race forward, leaping over every bush. The brush receded and the way became clear. Through the low ground cover, I could see the road. Beyond the rock barrier Naomi sat at the wheel.

In the cool recesses of the air-conditioned interior, I took a moment to catch my breath. "You won't believe what just happened."

"I think I will," she replied.

The obstruction at my right hip forced me to push off the seat and readjust my placement. In the throes of my adventure I hadn't been aware that I was carrying my camera. I never thought of taking a picture of the amazing images that had come to me.

We made it back in time for my past-life regression, but nothing could compare to Boynton Canyon. I had opened to a more sensitive and conscious place, more firmly grounded in the mystical realms. I had witnessed, firsthand, that Divine guidance isn't always subtle. Our spirit-guides can shape-shift in and out of our waking life at any time. When we step out of our own way, the messengers effortlessly step in.

CHAPTER 27

The Reconstruction Process

"**I** turned it over and realized it was the skull of a snake," I reported to the few gathered friends, days after my return from Sedona. Lori hadn't yet heard all the details of my Boynton Canyon adventure. As the group leaned in closer and I dramatically revealed more, she eagerly stood by me. Lori believed it was imperative to keep everyone engaged, and tonight I was particularly entertaining in her eyes, eyes that saw amusement as a valued quality.

When a few days had passed, however, her deeper distress over my experience had caused the familiar agitation she couldn't yet comprehend in herself. Lori tended to get edgy when I returned home from bodywork training and spiritual workshops, nervous about how I might be different after spending extended periods of time in the accelerated energy of consciously focused groups. "Out there," she called it. She was struggling to interface with me as I continued to change. The dream that stood ready would clearly reveal the issue we were not so delicately dancing around.

GUTTING AND RECONSTRUCTION
An old home has been bulldozed and is being rebuilt on its massive stone foundation. Lori and I are checking out the reconstruction. Oddly, it has been started at the top floor, a glorious open space that looks like a meditation room with

many adjacent spaces. Solidly built, this new construction is surrounded by windows and is flooded with light.

Only a few sets of temporary stairs precariously support the finished third floor. Haphazardly laid slats of wood are barely holding the first and second floors together. We have both chosen to go on, although getting to the new space will be dangerous for both Lori and me. We are carefully making our way up a staircase that has no handrails. I'm afraid we will fall and be hurt.

CHAPTER 28

Reconsidering The Wounding

"Amy," I called into the phone, "I have so much to tell you." I had found a friend who was as interested in studying dreams as I was, and we had begun meeting every few weeks to go over our latest and juciest entries. I had met Amy through Lori, when they were in culinary school together. They had practiced searing and sautéing techniques in our kitchen, but baking had become their primary interest. For an entire semester they kneaded and rolled out pastry dough, their aprons, hands, and faces covered in flour as they perfected their skills. "Tea time" always followed, and that's when Amy and I started talking about our dreams.

In answer to my call, our friend arrived at the front door carrying a tote bag heavy with books – a mobile library available for referencing and lending. I threw my arms around her, inhaling the sweet smell of the still-warm pastries in the white paper bag that peeked from her overstuffed tote.

"The bird shooting game" was my most recent dream, and its haunting message had brought back a nearly forgotten memory: a teenage experience I shared right up front.

"My cousin was visiting from Florida," I reported to Amy. "He found and brought home a pigeon that had been shot in the wing. Can you believe it? We spent all summer caring for it and watching it heal." I stopped to take a bite of a frosted sticky bun, closing my eyes to reflect. "Looking back, I wonder if the bird was a message trying to reach me all those years ago, a part of the puzzle."

I went on to share "the bird shooting game" with her, dramatically underscoring the helpless bird being rolled in, inside a cage, and the man at the center of our circle who raised his rifle for all to see. As I re-envisioned my fearful struggle to get away, I could feel the fear rising in me again, the loss of control. "I felt like the tiny bird was actually me," I finally admitted, sitting back on the couch, resting in the moment of reflection. "I couldn't avoid being shot."

"Parts of our spirit are often 'shot down' on our path to freedom," Amy gently commented after taking a long sip of chamomile tea. "I know I've lost parts of myself due to the dramas along the way. If it were my dream, I'd like to know more about the marksman, since he's responsible for the shooting."

"Yes, he's responsible," I mumbled. "I can see the marksman as my father. I'm still angry at him."

"Maybe our trip to Virginia Beach will bring some clarifying dreams," she encouraged. "Will you two be able to take the time off?" Our friend had just entered a whirlwind relationship with a man she was very serious about, but she was holding her vacation time open as a much needed feminine retreat for herself, Lori, and me.

"We wouldn't miss it."

FIVE A.M. WAS TOO EARLY for my partner, who had carried her pillow to the back seat of Amy's car and fallen asleep. "This is my favorite time of day," Amy said. "Every time I make this trip I think about how much I love to watch the sun rise. Amy had bought her condo a year ago, and had traveled to and from Virginia Beach so many times she didn't need a map or a navigator. There was nothing to distract us from the deeper conversations we enjoyed sharing.

"So, how's everything going with Brian?" I asked, curious to hear about their newly forming relationship.

"Good," she said, smiling in a way that let me know it was much better than good. "It's funny, as we ease into being together more, we're starting to see our differences." Amy thought for a moment. "I'm trying to stay open so I don't get judgmental with him. I'm noticing how easy it is for me to be judgmental."

"I know," I sighed, and shook my head at how well I knew. "When my judgment comes up, I get very resistant, and then I get angry at Lori. I know it works better if I let her be, but it's a constant practice for me to catch myself thinking she's not doing something the way I want her to, or the way I think it should be done, and then pull back from my old habit of saying so."

"It's funny, Amy turned her face away from the road for a second to make her point. "Our relationships look so different on the outside, but they really aren't different at all."

"No. When it comes to intimacy," I summarized, "gender has nothing to do with it. A good relationship takes work and two devoted partners, period."

The Chesapeake Bay Bridge Tunnel took us deep into the earth, under the salt water, into the depths. I closed my eyes and pondered last night's dream: *I'm lying on an operating table and a doctor is working on my heart. "Everything is all right now," he says.*

Such a positive bottom line had assured me: *whatever my heart's issues are, they're definitely in the process of being resolved.* I nodded off in the welcomed thought.

OUR LONG DAY OF TRAVELING didn't dampen our enthusiastic arrival at Amy's condo. A late supper led to tea in the living room, where our dear friend pulled her favorite oracle, the Medicine Cards, from her bookshelf.

"What would you like to know?" she asked as she shuffled the animal images well and spread them into a large circle, facedown. I crossed my legs and slid in closer.

"No spiritual stuff after ten," Lori insisted, reluctantly agreeing to pull just one card in answer to a pressing question. Amy looked to me and we smiled.

I pulled the Hawk that night, the messenger card. It put me on notice that life was sending me signals. I must be observant and look carefully at my surroundings. When we sat on the beach in the following days, Amy and I read to each other from books we had deliberately packed. "The soul" had stepped to the forefront of our conversations.

"Spiritual partners are able to distinguish personality from soul," I read to Amy from *The Seat of the Soul*, the book I couldn't put down. Lori stood, stretched, and adjusted her sun visor. She examined the flow of beachgoers before jogging off into the warm winds, tuning her ears to her own accelerated breath, grounding her stride in the wet sand.

ON AMY'S DECK WE SIPPED our morning coffee and tea. "Shrimp or crab?" Lori asked. "Asparagus or snow peas?" She and Amy were preparing our midweek home-cooked dinner.

"It all sounds good to me." I was half in their conversation and half in the blue sky, free of clouds.

Amy pulled a yellow gift bag from beneath her chair and held it between us. "I really enjoyed this book when I read it, so I bought you two a copy yesterday at the bookstore."

Its title alone, *Gift from the Sea,* made it the perfect souvenir, signed with love and a few lines honoring our week of deepening friendships. I quickly buried my nose in the delicate shell sketches that opened each chapter.

"I'm going to stay here if you don't mind," I called from the kitchen as Lori folded her grocery list. "I'm not up for shopping at the fish market." I was tapping the tea kettle to see if the water was still hot. When Amy grabbed her car keys I picked up the hardcover book and waved it in a thankful good-bye. The argonaut shell printed on its jacket, with a shadow in the shape of a woman's profile, drew my focused attention. There was something familiar about it.

To dig for treasures shows not only impatience and greed, but lack of faith, Anne Morrow Lindbergh wrote. *Patience, patience, patience, is what the sea teaches. Patience and faith. One should lie empty, open, choiceless as a beach – waiting for a gift from the sea.*

I slowly pulled the book away from my eyes. I was hearing something, no... someone. Her words were gentle and clear. I stretched my arm as far as it could reach, holding the first part of the emerging message in my mind as I tore a sheet of paper from the memo pad by the phone. Half of the contents of my purse fell to the floor in my attempt to extract a pen. The information was coming as fast as I could write:

"It's okay," she said. "This was done at a time when we were all in the energy of it. Life was forming us. We rallied to follow the path we were all meant to pursue. Our lives were full. We laughed.

We had our joy. We felt our sorrow and we felt the love." Her words were slowing down. *"Contact me whenever you need, dear Emma. Call upon me for guidance. I have never left your side. You are filled with my light. Memories may fade, but hold onto the bright images,"* her voice went on. *"Our life was not as painful as your perception of it.*

Release it. See the joy of our experience together. The gifts were many.

I love you."

My eyes filled and overflowed onto the paper, finally closing as I felt my mother's presence at my side and recognized the voice I had not heard for twelve and a half years. At the most unexpected moment, patience and faith had allowed this precious experience to come up from the undulating metaphysical waters like a gift from the sea, and it continued into another memory:

"Just try, Emma." My mother sounds exasperated. "I know it's hard, but try to do it, just like the book shows you."

All I want is to become an airline stewardess or a hairdresser, but my parents still insist that I complete the college preparatory courses. Tonight a headache accompanies me to bed.

I barely close my eyes before remembering the book report that is due.

Back down the attic stairs I shuffle through the dark, dropping on the floor of the hallway, leaning against the stair railing that leads to my parents' bedroom. I fall into tears.

My mother quietly emerges, lifts the glass door of the bookcase and invites me in. My watery vision focuses on the color of sand. I reach for the book with "the Sea" in its title.

I traded that hardcover book for a paperback, but hadn't forgotten the rare argonaut shell printed on its jacket. I finally recognized the title. *Gift from the Sea* had been my mother's book. Through this synchronistic channel she just handed it to me again.

The struggles my mother experienced on her soul's journey had a purpose and meaning for her. Whatever the reason for her selflessness, in her channeling of this truth to me, I could finally accept that she had chosen her own path. *Now, I have to let go of my judgments about her being a victim. To heal my own heart I must hold her unconditionally in mine, and as I do, my latest dream of a heart being healed will become manifest.*

The click of the key in the lock was followed by laughter and the chattering of my two closest friends. "You won't believe what just happened," I said as they dropped their bags on the table beside my open book. "I just had an incredible experience."

They both listened intently, and Amy gave me a hug before we dove into our next project, the preparation of a gourmet meal.

LORI'S MILD RESISTANCE DIDN'T DISTURB the flow of our glorious vacation or the intimate sharing between Amy and me. Spiritual insights continued to enlighten through the rest of the week. From under the striped umbrella I looked over my sunglasses on our final afternoon. "Wow, listen to this," I exclaimed, turning back to the previous page.

"I'm going for a run," Lori announced, turning away and adjusting her bathing suit.

"Is it after ten?" Amy playfully asked.

CHAPTER 29

Commitment

"The two of you can afford to buy a home," the real estate agent insisted – for the third week in a row – as she stepped out of my massage room at the chiropractic office and waved a "Think about it" goodbye.

The financial center of my brain had closed itself off when I was still in high school, from feeling my father's stress as he pondered over his ledger every April. Even as an adult, I had avoided thinking too seriously about money matters. Until now, I had made every life choice in answer to the "How does it feel?" question.

I waited until after dinner to introduce the idea to Lori. "We're throwing our rent out the window," I complained, finally realizing that this was true. "Buying a home would be a sound investment to make together," I added, to reinforce my case. I grabbed for the third reason like a juggler reaches for the largest, most colorful ball, tossing it into the air to increase the audience's interest. "I'm sure we can afford it."

Looking for a house didn't come from the mutual desire to expand our horizons together. The entire project grew from a thought that was both planted and watered by a third party's insistence. The real estate agent chattered through much of her half-hour massages until I agreed to take a look at what was available.

"This kitchen's too small for you, Lori," I prodded when we went to look at the raised ranch, still under construction, perfectly set into an established neighborhood. "Even without the cabinets you're going to feel cramped here," I insisted. I was walking in a circle, through the wide archway into our prospective living room, returning to the kitchen by way of the open doorway at the top of the front stairs. "There isn't any space we could expand into – and there's no dining room."

"But it's brand new, Emma." That was the most engaged comment my partner had offered on this matter so far. "And the location is perfect for both of us."

I stood on the threshold with arms crossed, wondering if I could adapt to the raised-ranch layout and somehow re-create the cozy feel of the little rented cape we would soon be leaving. "We're going to have the holidays here now." I was back in the living room, facing the opposite direction, extending my arms in front of me with palms turned inward, like a referee. We can add a second table and extend it into here." I was thinking aloud. "We'll have to make room for, let's see… twelve?"

"It won't be that often, Emma."

"I hope it will."

My interest wasn't centered on the area that was causing me to walk in circles. My spotlight rested on the ground-level space where I could clearly see my healing sanctuary with a private back entrance that opened to a thoughtfully designed landscape, abundantly rewarding the eyes for gazing into layers of perennial gardens. The lawnless wooded lot was already blooming in my mind. Birdfeeders stood along the gravel walkways that meandered through Stargazer lilies, Japanese iris, and an array of wildflowers. I could imagine a white concrete bench that offered a seat in the meditation corner for those who chose to rest in nature, eyes focused on a rotund sculpture of the Buddha. For summer nights, there would be a hand-laid brick patio surrounding a rustic rock-lined fire pit. Here, everything would effortlessly grow into perfection.

"If you like it, I like it," Lori insisted, when I questioned what she wanted to see on this blank canvas still smelling of varnished floors and vinyl windows. "But the driveway must be paved."

Aha! A passionate stance. This is what I was waiting for. Now I knew she was ready to sign the papers and make the move.

Through the following week of negotiations Lori remained on her mission to get the driveway paved. "He's not going to leave gravel on a hill," she shouted into the linguine that tumbled into our colander, steaming the front of her glasses. "He isn't going to avoid me by not returning my calls. I'm going over there tomorrow before work and straighten this out. And he's going to give us the lighting fixtures we want in the hallway too."

"Maybe we should just let this house go and keep looking." The drama was forcing me to retreat.

"I'll take care of this, Emma. In the morning."

Lori thrived in those areas of confrontation where I always tucked in my wings. She pushed and scrapped well. The following day she reared up and stood toe to toe with the greasy-haired, cigar-smoking contractor until she broke him. Not only was the driveway installed, but we were given permission to choose all the lighting fixtures throughout the upstairs of the house at no additional cost.

I did what I do best: pulled a rabbit out of the hat. We closed off a coat closet to add space for a pantry, had the small bathrooms tiled to make them more elegant and inviting. My gardens began to bloom, well into the fall.

This was our way of honoring our relationship the best way we could. After all, marriage wasn't an option for those of us who chose the alternative path. In this significant move we were revealing to the world our commitment to be a couple, serious about our life partnership. I fully believed we were. That house had given us a brand-new beginning – one we were both invested in – and I saw it as an opportunity to deepen our committed path.

As Thanksgivings and Christmases came and went, I grew close to Lori's growing nieces and nephews. In the summer they came for sleep-overs and in the late fall we started our week-end "craft days." I spread out paints, beads, glue guns, wood-burning tools, and my sewing machine so we could create Christmas presents for every member of Lori's family. We had a separate wrapping day, where we recycled last year's Christmas cards and made our own tags.

Lori and I started hosting Christmas, Easter, and birthday dinners together. We were getting the whole system down. We had all the plates, all the serving dishes, and all the tablecloths for both tables. This new home is what ushered us into a fresh spectrum of opportunity and growth together. I had become an integral part of her family as she was becoming an integral part of mine.

CHAPTER 30
The Gift From Will

There's a knock at the door and Will, a massage school teacher, hands me a birthday gift. His offering is not wrapped in colorful paper and ribbon but is presented in two corrugated cardboard boxes. From one, I remove white copier paper stapled together in different packets. What kind of present is this?

I curiously scan the first chapter, but don't understand what the transcript is about. No guests have gathered. The private opening is between Will and me. He is standing as a guardian over the boxes and, even though I can't surmise what any of this means, I feel it is very important to him.

"This is great," I tell him. "Thank you for your beautiful gift."

"My manuscript has arrived! I have WILLed it into being." I scribbled on the page across from the description of my dream. Without another thought, I pulled a chair up to the computer and placed my fingers on the keypad:

Where do I begin a story that holds no structured form in my mind? What words can bind together a narrative I have been told I will write and am expected to pull from an indecipherable manuscript given in a dream? What do you expect me to create from a pile of beliefs, struggles, recollections, and dreams that have formed me?

I held the moment open, waiting for the answer:

My mother's passive attitude… I hated it. My father pushed her like a workhorse and she never complained. His jokes and thoughtless remarks about my slowly developing breasts were inappropriate! Mean! Destructive! Why didn't she stop him?

I'm furious with you, Dad. Why did *I* find the pornography you kept in a drawer we had all entered? Another secret *I* exposed. You asked me to babysit for Harriet's daughter so she could sing in your choir. Did you think I believed you had spent all those late nights rehearsing her parts? Until midnight?

My frenetic tapping obliterated any subtle guidance as I invited the anger and provoked the words I had never said out loud. My inner victim pecked at the keys like a hungry vulture, pulling out the entrails of furious recollection.

I never should have married him!

I don't think I can write about THIS. Over unformed words my fingers lifted. One hand retreated into my lap and the other rested above it, like a delicate porcelain cup in a saucer, containing my steaming rage.

CHAPTER 31

Lake Placid

"There are grocery stores in Florida," I teased, as Lori attempted to jam the canvas "food bag" under her seat. It was another thing to lug along, but upon landing I would be grateful for the organic selections and bottles of water that were neatly packed inside. The projected storm had become a dusting that glistened on the runway. The pilots sat like two figurines in an undisturbed snow globe, unaffected by the thumping of carry-on bags being thrust into overhead compartments. To avoid watching the flotation-device and oxygen-mask demonstrations, my partner pulled out a magazine and started flipping through. When racing engines propelled us backward, she reached for my hand.

"I hope you're okay with making our trip to the villa at the beginning of the week," I re-ran the idea past Lori, once the beverage cart was rumbling down the aisle.

She smiled and took my hand again. "Not a problem," she promised.

Until Dad and Margaret made their move, I didn't know there was a Lake Placid in Florida. Adventurous vacation destinations, such as Chitzanitza and Negril, had now been replaced by predictable returns to Sanibel Island and Lake Placid.

My father was finished with making car trips to Massachusetts and back. "If you want to see us, you'll have to come down here," he insisted. The inescapable hand of time was pulling him into Alzheimer's. Slowly numbing his mind. Obscuring his memory.

I was staring into space, drifting to the back porch of the villa we would soon enter. My most recent memory was ripe, ready to be plucked from the vine that held every one of my past experiences with my father… ready to be tasted again:

"Our life is good," Dad is saying as Margaret nods her head from the doorway. She has taken drink orders and turns to head toward the kitchen. To avoid the discomfort of sitting with Dad, Lori has tagged along.

He's really mellowed in the past twenty years, I'm thinking, as he and I look through the porch screens and beyond the second fairway. Eighteen-wheelers fly by the little paradise that quietly protects the elderly in a safe cocoon. We are both waiting for a thought to emerge. Having lost the ability to tell a joke about anything that comes up in conversation, my father can't enter one now without losing his train of thought.

"Jonathan will be getting married next year," I announce.

"You're talking about someone I should know, but I don't remember who he is," Dad responds.

"Jonathan," I repeat. "Your grandson, Jonathan."

"Oh yes. I can't place him, but I know who you mean."

I find it a comfort to watch my father float in his vulnerability, forced to remain in the present moment with each spoken word. It releases me from my relentless judgments.

He crosses his legs and allows his leathery shoulders to drop deeper into the back cushion. Clouded eyes remain focused on the re-lit cigar stub he places to his lips. The inhalation of smoke inspires him to speak. "If I were to walk out onto the golf course today," he says, breaking off the ember in the ashtray, "and I never came back" – he looks directly into my eyes – "I would be at peace."

My heart opens a little more. I'm breathing into his words. "I'm really glad to hear that, Dad. I'm grateful you could share that with me."

The tray overflowing with snacks and drinks precedes Margaret and Lori's energetic conversation about cheddar and horseradish dips and Margaret's favorite crackers. Melting ice cubes float on the surface of his glass as Dad turns toward the sunset once again.

"ARE YOU OKAY?" LORI'S VOICE broke through my concentrated stare. She knew I was apprehensive about this year's visit. "He was very accepting of us," she reminded me, taking a sip of water. "Remember the day he said he had never seen you smile like you have since we've been together?"

That moment was one I couldn't forget. Since then he hadn't remarked about such things. When I called now, and Margaret handed him the phone, he was barely cognizant of which daughter he was talking to.

We planned to stay in the villa without a break – not even for our usual trip out to dinner. Any change in the environment would be too confusing for Dad. His abusive outbursts had sent him out of the dentist's office without resolving his dental pain. Margaret faithfully prepared him soft foods at every meal.

Our upcoming visit was pre-scripted. When we got around to recounting our latest adventures, Dad wouldn't retain them. A few hours into our stay, he would begin asking when we were planning to leave. My heart would struggle to remain open as he snapped at Lori for drinking from her water bottle. I would hold my tongue.

On our second afternoon, Lori pushed to move on. Like the eroded underpinnings of a stilt house, my firm stand had loosened in the quickening currents. This time I drove through torrential rains that slowed traffic nearly to a halt, holding back my guilt at leaving so soon, as lightning filled the sky.

The window of opportunity had closed long ago, leaving unanswered questions floating beyond my reach. To resolve any issues I continued to harbor, I would have to do the work on my own, on myself. Like my mother, my father was now in a place that I could connect with only on the level of dreams.

CHAPTER 32
Surrender

"Margaret had a heart attack." Gina forced her words into the phone as if the emergency had sucked the breath out of her. "Seth is flying down from Seattle and I'm heading out tonight."

As I pictured Margaret's only child flying across the country to be at his mother's side and our youngest sister heading for the airport, I erupted with questions. "What about Dad? What if we have to put him on a plane – or even in a car – to bring him to Massachusetts?" I asked when Kathleen called.

"He'll never let us take him," she replied matter-of-factly, before we slid into a pondering silence. "Remember how he reacted when Peg and Doug visited last summer? Dad sat in the back seat, repeating over and over again that he knew they were taking him somewhere to lock him up. Until they returned home he refused to hear anything different."

My mind could barely find a place to rest between the pictures of our father's fragile vulnerabilities and our list of options to assist him.

Peg's commonsense response was the one I most needed to hear. "He'll be angry, Emma, but he won't remember who brought him here." We all agreed that without Margaret to buffer, Dad would make things difficult at best.

As Seth's mother lay unconscious, connected to oxygen and intravenous tubes, he was preparing to give the doctor permission to remove all life support. "He's going to give her another day," Gina reported from the Florida kitchen, "but the prognosis isn't good. Her lungs are filling up, Emma…" Gina's vioce muffled. "He just came in. I don't want to upset him any more than he already is. He's looking for something in his suitcase. I think he's burning some kind of herbs in the back yard."

"A sacred ritual," I confirmed. We knew he was praying for guidance on his mother's fate in ways he had learned from the Lakota tribe. Several years before, a denied request to photograph a tribal ceremony had deepened his interest in their well-protected culture and beliefs. He had since studied their traditions, attended their sweat lodges, and sought their help when he was sick.

At sunrise the next morning he stood on the low cut grass, faced the four directions again, then honored earth and sky. Gina was up. As she stirred her coffee she stepped onto the back porch and squinted, trying to decipher what the tiny figure kneeling on the ground at the other side of the fairway was doing. When he repacked his medicine bundle, she dropped into the soft cushions of our father's chair.

Seth's dark eyes, which normally expressed a gentle vulnerability, approached her with an illuminated strength. He whispered, not to awaken Dad, "If nothing has changed, I'll give them permission to take her off. I have to honor her wishes."

As his car pulled out of the driveway Gina called me again. "I'm glad I'm not responsible for making this decision," she sighed, before we fell into a wordless stretch, listening to each other's quickened breathing as we waited for a thought that might be helpful. "I'll call you as soon as I know anything," she finally said.

I hung up the phone and stayed near it, imagining Margaret's face lying on the pillowcase like a smooth white stone. Heavy. Motionless.

Cold. I knew Seth and his mother were meant to experience this decisive moment together, but that couldn't lift the weight of it. When he returned to the villa he told Gina he was tempted to believe that there was still life inside of her, aching to return. He prayed for his mother to hear and feel his presence as he sat in the timeless space that he believed could allow for the unimaginable to occur. And amazingly, it did. Her paper-thin eyelids slowly raised halfway, then closed again. His mother's emerging presence delivered her from the darkness like a precious birth, and she extended her hand to him.

In this immense time of need, the Native American spirits my father disavowed all his life came to retrieve his loving partner from between the worlds, so they would be blessed with a longer life together. When I received the thrilling news, they passed the phone from hand to hand until Dad eagerly took the receiver.

"How are you doing?" I asked.

"Great. We're having a pow wow."

Seth had lit some sage and had joined my father in smoking cigars, an unspoken tobacco offering to spirit. My father joyfully reported once again what he had already forgotten he had shared: "We're having a pow wow."

Two years later, when I answered Kathleen's call, this memory was a raw reminder. "I just spoke with Gina," she said. "Margaret collapsed. Dad ran for help and someone called the ambulance." I knew it was my turn to make the trip.

"We're going to give it a few days," Kathleen quickly reported back, after her conversation with Peg. "A nurse will be coming in every day from eleven a.m. until seven. The neighbors are close friends. They'll check in on him. We'll wait and see how Margaret does."

I wasn't sure how I felt about waiting, but I agreed to be the third daughter to call and check in on him, on Monday night.

"I don't know where my family is," he spilled into the phone. Where's my honey?" Any response to his pleading for answers he would immediately forget.

"We're on our way, Dad." I was shaking. "Are you ready for bed? When you go to bed and wake up, I'll be there. I'm on my way."

PEG AND I NEARLY RAN from our meeting point to the baggage claim, regurgitating the most recent piece of information and feeding bits of it to each other like mother birds to ravenous chicks. The health care provider hadn't been to the villa for the past two days because Dad told her he had a gun and was planning to shoot himself and make it look like she had done it.

"Does he still have the rifle?" I raised my voice over the rumbling luggage return.

"I wouldn't put it past him to have carried it to Florida and hidden it away in the closet somewhere," Peg said, her stressed imagination running on overdrive.

"Do you think he could remember where it was, if he did have it?"

"Probably not," she said, trying to sound hopeful.

"Peg! He forgets where the ice is when he goes to the kitchen to make himself a drink."

Thoughts of Uncle Martin and my father as young men riding horses, wanting to be cowboys, conjured up the vision of Dad holding that well-guarded rifle high. Both brothers had shared the belief that they would "take care of things" if they "became a problem" to others. Dad had repeatedly expressed to us as he got older, "I'll never be a burden to anyone. You don't need to worry." I was beginning to wish I had asked for specific details.

"Where have you been?" Dad opened the screen door, looking fragile and frightened. "I didn't know where my family was. Where have you been?" He was completely lost, his mind covered in a web of confusion. Peg and I kept glancing into each other's eyes for strength. Tears filled his as we made every attempt at recovering his security. He agreed to shower and eat only after being given the promise that he could see Margaret.

Connected to intravenous tubes and oxygen, she lay in the same bed – in the same intensive care unit – Gina had photographed two years before. At the time, that picture of Dad, sitting at Margaret's side, was placed on his kitchen table, where Gina could hand it to him as a reminder that he had just visited her.

Unable to speak, Margaret smiled as the three of us walked through the door together.

"You look beautiful," Dad called out, shuffling to her side. He lifted his hand and softly touched the blackened bruises that surrounded the intravenous needles. Peg pushed a chair in close behind him, and he rested his tired body in his sweetheart's presence.

"She's amazing," the nurse remarked. "We never expected her to come around like this."

But Margaret was far from coming home. As the days rolled on, Peg and I wore out our repetitious conversations over what we would do when this week came to an end.

"Do you think you could find us a place?" Margaret's tired voice murmured when all but one tube had been removed. She was pulling me toward her with a surprisingly firm grip.

"Who should we talk to?" The adrenaline was coursing through my veins.

"Beth, in the office." I couldn't believe what I was hearing.

"Kathleen!" I nearly yelled into the phone. "Margaret has asked us to find her an apartment in assisted living. I know. She's never even considered it. We're still in shock. I hope we can pull it off in the next three days."

PEG AND I KICKED INTO overdrive, tossing and turning through the night, waking up and making lists that were almost identical. We left for Sebring as the sun was rising.

"We can take a look at all three places," Peg assured me, "and get home before Dad rolls out of bed."

She was right. He wouldn't get up until after eleven, and by ten o'clock we had made our choice and stood over the papers that would legally bind them to their new living space.

"We need Margaret's okay," Peg reminded as she handed the hospital number to the head of admissions and pointed to the phone.

"Margaret." The tubes had been removed. She answered the call. "It's Emma."

"I just called you at the villa, Emma." Her voice was hoarse. "I woke your Dad."

"Oh, no." I looked to Peg in exasperation. "Well, we agreed on your top choice. It's brand new. Beautiful. There's a fountain in the lobby and an Alzheimer's unit in the same building, if Dad needs it later on. I think you'll feel at home here. In time there will be more tenants. I'm going to hand you over to Gail. She'll explain everything to you and ask a few questions." With this abrupt explanation, we grabbed the paperwork, handed the phone to the administrator, and dashed to the parking lot. I think we made the thirty-five-minute trip back to the villa in about twenty-three.

"Where have you been?" Dad was outside, in front of his neighbor's, wandering. "I've been looking for you." Behind my frenzied frustration, my heart was breaking.

"I'll help you find a nice shirt to wear to the hospital," Peg said, rushing him into his bedroom. "Margaret's waiting for you."

MY FATHER SAT AT MARGARET'S side while we delivered the signed papers, shopped, installed a small refrigerator, and threw a new set of sheets into the wash. A neighbor pulled up in a truck as we returned to the villa for some essentials. The gray-haired man offered to transport some furniture.

"Unbelievable," we echoed, on our way back into the house to earmark the TV, couch, and Dad's reclining chair. As Peg and I made our final run to the new apartment to stock the refrigerator and bathroom shelves, my mind offered up a picture of them, clinging to each other in the private room Margaret had occupied for less than twenty-four hours. There seemed no way her doctor would allow her to leave. She hadn't eaten a full meal since she entered the hospital.

At three p.m. we lifted Margaret from the wheelchair into the back seat next to her oxygen tank. A few breathless words to thank us for everything triggered her familiar coughing and choking. My hands gripped the steering wheel as I glanced at my sister. She had already passed along the box of tissues.

"We really fooled them, didn't we, Ed?" Margaret insisted on talking through another coughing spell, with Peg twisting around from the front seat to assist. "The doctor wouldn't sign my release papers until I ate my lunch, but when he stepped out, I gave it to your father!"

Oblivious to the trick they had played, Dad stared out at the passing scenery, making the whole thing feel even more surreal. The double lines marked our way like the yellow-brick road to the Emerald City. We prayed for a safe delivery.

Peg filled two disposable cameras with pictures for everyone back home. As she carefully snapped away at her documentary, Dad lifted a framed photograph from the table.

"This is ours," he said.

Peg and I pulled each of them tightly to us – clinging – like the flowered magnets clung to their new refrigerator, and in compulsory surrender we dragged our tired bodies back to the car, and the villa, for four hours of sleep.

Adrenaline propelled Peg and me north again, to our separate flights heading to separate states. When I finally took my seat and buckled myself in, I drifted off to the contented place of accomplished wishes for the entire family.

"I'M DOING MUCH BETTER," MARGARET's triumphant voice sounded revived when she called, a few months later, to give each of us the news. "I'm getting around well and feeling good. There aren't many new residents in the complex yet. I really missed my friends so they moved us back into the villa."

I gripped the phone.

She went on to explain how her faithful friends rallied to bring the two of them "home" to a renewed freedom, while four daughters and a son sat crushed at the loss of what we had believed to have been security and peace of mind. In the next crisis with no in-house support, we would be in the same place, orchestrating from afar.

We exhausted ourselves for a week. What was the lesson in that? I silently ranted when I hung up the phone.

Expectations, was my immediate answer. *Disappointment comes from my own expectations.*

What we put in place was necessary in the moment. Beyond that, it was their journey to navigate, as long as they could navigate it. For my heart to stay open, I had to let go of my need to control and my underlying fear.

JOURNEY OF SISTERS - ENLIGHTENMENT ABOUT FEAR

I'm on a large ship with Peg, Gina, and Kathleen. We have placed our baggage below and have returned to the deck, a bare wooden floor with a flimsy woven railing around its perimeter. It feels like a precarious position for the travelers on deck, but I feel extremely grateful to be here.

"*Once you are on this ship, I'm not responsible for any of you,*" *the captain says, taking my ticket and tearing it into pieces. He dramatically throws the proof of my being on the ship over the side.*

"*Now, I know why I'm here,*" *I say to the heavens.* "*To be responsible for myself and to let go of my fears.*"

I look to the stars and realize the time it has taken for the planets to align in such a way that would allow my sisters and me to embark on this journey together. We have waited for a long time.

CHAPTER 33
Detachment

"If it were my dream...." Amy jumped right in. We had been meeting every other week to look at our journal entries. "I would be very concerned about their welfare."

She was referring to the brilliantly colored butterflies, twelve inches across, that had been packed into a brown paper bag and dropped at my feet by a gray-haired man.

A lot had happened in this dream. A young girl leaned on one of the butterflies as I attempted to get a photograph of her sitting beside it. By the time I pulled her away, the butterfly had transformed into a folded paper. I unfolded it and the butterfly was inside, but one of its wings had become detached.

"Specifically," Amy re-formed her words, "I'm concerned about the welfare of the butterfly in its unfolding."

"It can't fly on one wing," I went for the obvious. "One needs to be balanced in order to take flight. I don't know if the wing has been broken on the left or the right; a logical or intuitive aspect, receptive or assertive quality, that I'm not connected to. I see the butterfly as the symbol of transformation." I let the free association flow. "The unfolding of my book is assisting me in my spiritual transformation."

"And, in the process, according to your dream," Amy added, "the detached wing is being revealed. There is definitely something in here for me about detachment."

"I've been consciously working with this broken-winged spirit. The bird, and now the butterfly. I feel annoyed at the man's irresponsible handling of these unique butterflies. I'm angry at the woman who turns her back, and the child who is more concerned with having her picture taken than being careful of this beautiful creature."

"In my dream," Amy gently reminded me, "all three characters are parts of myself."

"Mmm," I said, not yet ready to look at her helpful input. I was actually thinking about something completely different, another dream symbol. "When I involve myself with pulling the young girl away from the butterfly, I miss the opportunity to take her picture. This is another recurring issue in my dreams," I sighed, dropping my chin into my hand. "Without 'getting the picture,' how can I heal this broken part of myself? And until I connect to both of my wings, how can any new creative projects take off and be successful?"

To THE SOUND OF APRIL rains I continued to ponder the plight of my dream butterflies as Lori and I took turns standing over the warm ironing board, pressing wrinkles from clothing that had been packed away for seven months.

Our thoughts of returning to Lake Placid weren't as upbeat this year. We were uneasy about our imagined three-day stay with Dad and Margaret and, as soon as we arrived, we began dancing around the man who couldn't remember who we were talking about. He had lost his spark that connected us. It was as if the deeper part of him had permanently moved into another room. I could barely recall the feel of his past hugs and the sound of his old laughter.

From his involuntary detachment, an agitated bark occasionally escaped, reminding us that a piece of his cantankerous judgment still resided within. As the shell of my father sat on the porch, lighting a cigar stub and letting it go out again, my partner and I took a walk on the golf course to ease the pain.

"When did you girls say you were leaving?"

"In a few minutes, Dad. We just have to pack the car."

In the days that followed, Lori and I drew closer. Our tanned bodies met in the passion that grew from the luxurious freedom of walking in the warm ocean air on silvery white sands and being served delicious meals. Present in every moment, we laughed, nurtured each other, and played.

We returned home to the new house with my expanding perennial gardens, a massage room set up and ready to be used at any time, our secure jobs, and our supportive families, but we still found reasons to justify and continue our arguments. Although they were less frequent, and I was keenly aware of my holding back from reacting for as long as I could, I was still getting hooked.

THE DANGEROUS SLIDE RIDE

Men have lined up at the foot of a ladder leading to a huge slide. At the end of the slide no one has gotten off, so about ten men are sitting up against each other, front to back, in a partially reclined position.

The man at the top jumps up, like he's doing a swan dive, then slides head first, belly down, crashing head to head with the man who is last in line, at the bottom. There is a horrendous crack as all the craniums bang together. I'm shocked and disturbed at this dangerous sport. The men aren't even wearing helmets, and I think this is crazy.

The diver flips over to join the others in the reclined position. They are waiting for the next man to dive down the slide.

THE CALAMITOUS SLIDE-AND-CRASH GAME HORRIFIED me. I was present, sensitive, and calm in my work and with friends, but privately I continued to bang heads with Lori. I dove into each crashing blow.

Repetitious "banging" and the fact that no one was "getting off" likened the activity to participating in addictive sexual encounters for the orgasmic feelings they created. Could I be addicted to the replaying of our dramatic skirmishes for the adrenaline rush?

My dreams, my writing, and even my father's senility had provided me with an alternative that I still couldn't quite "get." How many times did I need to be handed the word "detachment" before I actually understood it? Integrated it? Who would explain to me how I might practice letting go without feeling that I was giving in? I wasn't going to repeat my mother's pattern. I had to speak my mind and not back down. Sadly, yelling still felt safer than silence.

CHAPTER 34
Barrier Of Stone

A s I documented my "head-banging" dream on the computer, I wished that personal power issues could be resolved more simply and change could happen without resistance. In our attempts to get our needs met, Lori and I had played the full scale of options. I had tried giving us space, locking doors, running away, screaming louder, and being silent. I contemplated leaving but was afraid that if I didn't work this out with her, I would run into it again, in my next relationship. *If this is why we are in the "earth school," to learn these lessons, then I am committed to it. Help us to see how we can break our old habits and live more harmoniously.*

The heat of summer always smoothed our rough edges, but this year a percolating pot still sat on the back burner. Packing for our Rhode Island vacation was just another distraction from our urgent need to talk. On the first night we arrived, an opportunity was offered up in the form of a dream:

CRASHING TOWER WINDOW

Lori and I are sitting on a lush green lawn, observing an ancient tower that has a single window at the top. The huge pane of glass falls out of its opening and has begun a slow descent, back and forth toward the ground. As it gets closer I am afraid for Lori's safety, but when it hits and shatters, she is unaffected by it.

> *A house is about to be built for Lori and me, on the same*
> *property, but there is a construction problem. A gully of pure*
> *rock needs to be blasted through before a foundation can be set*
> *in place.*
> *I don't know if this is possible.*

LORI LED THE WAY OVER the warm sand to our favorite spot at the end of the public beach. I had slipped my journal into the woven purple bag that now sat at my side. As she took her jog, I flipped through the pages to refresh my memory. The cold salt water invigorated my intent when I joined her in a swim. After we had dried off and she opened up the cooler, I moved a little closer.

"I had a dream last night," I gently began. "I'd like to share it with you if you'd like to hear it."

"Sure," Lori agreed, a pile of fresh cherries in her hand. Even if she had no feedback to give, she understood it always helps to have a witness for our important dreams.

"I'm concerned about our relationship," I told her, after leaving a space to take in my dream. "There's something here about a shattering window of opportunity and new foundations. Most importantly, I've been thinking about this layer of rock that needs to be blasted through."

We both knew what this metaphor was about. "We have such differences of opinion, Lori. I don't see how we can break through this pattern. I'm afraid we can't do it."

Our most recent blowup had led us to the burdensome truth that we have opposing definitions of "acceptable"and "unacceptable." "When we can't agree at such a basic level," I had defeatedly put out, "how can we stop these petty arguments?" At the end of that conversation we remained teetering on a faultline, waiting, I suppose, for the inevitable earthquake.

As I attempted once again to explain our predicament, Lori stared through her sunglasses at a sailboat heading for the thin line where the sea meets the sky. The tiny silhouette had reached the defined edge that was once believed to be the end of the world. In the rumbling of the incoming tide, I felt the possibility of the boat suddenly plummeting like a wooden barrel thrown over Niagara Falls.

"I don't know if we can change our power struggle mindset, or intense communications, Lori." Her eyes remained on the tiny boat. "We've exhausted ourselves. I don't think I can withstand your resistance anymore. I don't know if I should stay in this relationship."

Over the edge. The point of no return.

"You are the resistant one!" she snarled. "You resist my family. You resist my outgoing nature."

"That's not true. You don't accept me for who I am. You judge everything I do. You can't stay present with me."

"We're going home, right now! If you're leaving me, we're going now."

I DIDN'T WANT TO LEAVE her, but my voice silenced itself as Lori tore the umbrella from the sand and frantically stuffed it into its protective sleeve. The identical emotion – fear – had thrown us both onto the familiar treadmill of our old patterning.

The wind broke her sentences apart as I swiftly folded up our chairs and towels, hoping to avoid any humiliating public confrontation, but shaded eyes remained on us.

IN THE BLISTERING SILENCE SHE drove us back to the cottage. We gathered our belongings and entered the back door. *Time,* I kept praying. *Give us more time.*

"I can never come here again. You've ruined everything!" she yelled.

On the second floor, on a handmade quilt, I found comfort in the fetal position. Like a viral infection, my own raging emotions were in full circulation. I breathed into the painful areas to release the negativity while Lori raced through the rooms below, empowered by the roar of the vacuum cleaner. When my body calmed, I sat on the edge of the bed and stared out the window.

We had held each other on this pier, paddled kayaks over the gentle waves, and taken tender walks along this beach. Why couldn't we have the challenging conversations without fighting? I needed to understand. I leaned toward the window and gazed across the salt pond that sparkled with possibilities. A pair of swans swam toward our shore. *They mate for life.*

Her slow and evenly paced footsteps ascended the planked stairs. I waited until she sat down to turn and face her.

"I'm sorry, Emma."

She reached for me and our hearts opened. We held each other until we breathed as one. There was no reason to run away. This was the place we needed to be to work with our fears, in the healing natural sanctuary we treasured.

CHAPTER 35

First Words Revealed

I walk into a public bathroom and a wolf lunges from behind the stall door, snarling in my face. I stand firm. I know I need to face my fears, no matter what the outcome. A ferocious energy builds inside me, causing me to growl into the wolf's drooling snout. He slowly backs off, transforming into a stuffed animal. I grab it with my teeth, shake it, and toss it to the floor. When I walk through another door, I am in a large bedroom. On the floor in front of me is a bound publication. "Ah," a gentle female voice says from behind me, "you found your book."

I open to the first page to see if I can read what has been written. The first two lines are in bold print and I can read them perfectly.

I FOUND MY BOOK IN the bedroom, the place where intimacy unfolds. Although I couldn't recall the first two lines after waking from the dream, I knew that on some level, this book had already been written, and it was going to entail much more than I first expected. My willful seeking was going to take me to a place of releasing, facing my fears, and recounting my most personal experiences.

I had a hard time seeing myself as the ferocious wolf but looked seriously at his appearance in my dream. Fearlessly taking charge had caused him to soften and fall at my feet. Since the dream had also placed my book at my feet, I felt that my response to aggressive behavior was related to its final content.

With complete trust in the process, I added the dream to my growing pile of writing.

CHAPTER 36
The Collective Opportunity

"You can leave me here as long as you like," I told Dr. Chen as my eyelids dropped and the lights dimmed. I could tell from the prickly sensation at the points of his well-placed acupuncture needles that awakened energy was stirring.

When he closed the door behind him, I noticed, in the waiting room on the other side of the wall, a television commentary had started. There were a few health videos set out for patients, but I had never seen anyone sit and watch them. The distracting chatter suddenly dissolved and the gentle music of flutes and ocean waves poured into the tiny room from a speaker in the corner.

When the needles had been removed, I dressed and passed the silenced television without a thought. At the front desk I fumbled through my purse for my checkbook.

"Did you hear about the towers?" the receptionist asked, glancing by me into the next room. My puzzled look answered her question. "They hit both of the World Trade Center towers."

Who are THEY? I wondered as I signed my name and tore out my payment.

When I turned, cameras were extending their lenses into flames and black smoke. Thick gray ash hung in streets that were filling with droves of fire trucks. Choppy camera footage carried us back to the windows. I was too far away to see that it wasn't just scorched debris that was falling downward. People were jumping to their deaths.

"Say a prayer," I murmured.

PROTECTED BY A PEACEFUL BALANCE, I walked to my car, stood at the door, and closed my eyes, allowing the images to trickle back into my stilled mind. What came to me was a dream. Not one of my own; a woman at a recent workshop had shared it with the group:

"I'm in a large city," the woman had said, "and it's been leveled by destruction. Smoke is billowing into the sky. I'm walking with others from the smoldering ashes into the light, beyond the destruction, to green fields that I can clearly see ahead of us. When I wake, I have the feeling that all is perfect and divinely planned."

Everyone in the class had sat in silence after the woman spoke.

"This is a *Prophetic Dream*," our teacher had said.

I couldn't understand what the soft-spoken woman could possibly be predicting. Here we stood, in the middle of her dream today.

THE WORLD WOKE UP IN the days following 9/11. An undisputed filter was set in place and mindless television programming stopped. We were all staring into the images of metal frames twisted and broken, the bones of the towers that had been pulverized by two catastrophic implosions. The gaping fire-filled hole in the Pentagon flashed across our screens between constant replays of the first plane's impact, and then the second. Courageous voices recorded on cell phones reported to us, over and over, the final moments before the fourth plane and all of its travelers dove to the earth, leaving behind only a deep, charred void.

I sat beside Julie in meditation, sending light to the souls who were hanging in limbo, unable to separate from the earth plane. *We must use these images as messages of healing,* I thought. *Now, we will make conscious choices.* I was convinced this level of collective shock would be enough to push us forward. *We can create a new reality.*

"I wish it didn't take tragic events to create core change," I lamented to my clients, in those numbing days. "I hope this opens our hearts and brings us together."

The war generated by this act of violence and our collective fears brought a stunning realization forward. I couldn't ignore my personal part in the human dilemma playing out before us: *Meeting aggression with retaliation only fortifies our differences and increases the stakes. If our outer world is a reflection of our inner conflicts, which I believe to be true, then, for the good of the world, it is imperative that we take responsibility for making peace within ourselves.*

CHAPTER 37
Voices Of The Sisterhood

"We're moving back to Massachusetts, Emma!" Peg's excitement poured into the phone. "Doug has decided to retire from dentistry. We really want to be nearer to the family, and Doug wants to be woodworking full time. He wants to start selling his art."

"Wow, I can't believe it! It's been so long. It'll be hard to leave your friends."

"I know, but it's time. Keith is heading to college. My baby."

"It's a big step, Peg, but I have to be honest, it'll be nice to have you closer."

Their new home was less than half an hour away, close enough to meet up for an occasional lunch, but Peg and I didn't connect in that way. I have to take responsibility for my own part in it. I didn't make the time, either, not at the beginning. Like the goldfish kept in a fish bowl for too long a time, when Peg was moved, she didn't extend farther than her old boundaries. She set up tennis, bridge, and her personal-trainer dates in her familiar pattern. The nearly undetectable beginning of our family's deep shift was meant to come about slowly.

On their first Massachusetts Thanksgiving, we all drove to Peg and Doug's new home, which stood at the top of a hill where she could see the sunsets from her front porch. This had been one of my sister's top priorities, along with designated areas in the yard where she could dig in the dirt and plant her flowers. Doug took each of us through his basement "playspace," where he had begun "making sawdust" with his ever reliable "other partner," a wood-turning lathe with a fourteen-inch bowl capacity. "It was a bitch getting it in here," he said with a laugh. "I'd rather have replaced a few crowns than try to lift this up and squeeze it through both doorways, but my brother came over. It's like childbirth. We're slowly forgetting the pain."

Their new dining room was nearly the size of Kathleen's. We all squeezed in, taking hands to sing grace before diving into our favorite foods. Jon opened a bottle of dry red wine that tasted to me like it had been infused with tobacco. I stayed with my gin and tonic.

After clearing the table, we huddled around the fireplace that crackled with the anticipation of a Girl Scout campfire. "We have to plan a weekend." Kathleen held up her mug of black coffee in a toast to her idea. "A sisters' weekend. Just the girls."

We were sitting closer than I had realized, in the warm configuration of our family members. We were as close, yet separate, as the sections of a plump, ripe grapefruit. For the first time in ages – maybe the first time ever – I was feeling the integrity of our tribe of sisterhood that had grown from the open attic bedrooms that had bonded us. Gina was already dreaming up a Cape Cod getaway. Peg and Doug had a timeshare we could adapt to our arising needs. I wrapped an arm around Kathleen. Peg wrapped an arm around me. Gina squeezed our cluster tight. "This summer." Kathleen wanted a signed statement.

"This summer," we all agreed.

"So…" I eased into the next area of interest I needed to address while the timing was right, "I've been writing a book."

"Really?" The stereophonic reply vibrated through my courage. *The dancer now writing?*

What's it about?" Gina asked as she picked up a bowl of chocolate-covered mints and offered one to Peg.

"Well, it started out as a book about dreams, and how they guide us toward healing; but I can't write about healing without revealing the wounding. So… in order to do that, I need to talk about our childhood." I cleared my throat. "And some of Dad's less positive characteristics."

"I know you have a lot of issues with him, Emma." Sadness softened Kathleen's voice as she raised a hand to Gina's sweet offering. "No thanks." Her eyes rested squarely on mine. "You and Dad have bumped heads a lot." Still, the softened voice. "I think you've been angry at him."

I reached for a mint and bit into the soft center, holding my comments until she was finished.

"I don't see our childhood from the same perspective as you," Kathleen continued. Her tone was strengthening. "I hope your writing will include some of our happier times."

"I think it does." *Doesn't it?* "Actually, I'm still gathering information. The story hasn't been fully developed. I haven't found an ending or even a clear form. I keep dreaming that I'm making a quilt with three-dimensional sections. I'm trying to fit together cutouts that are in odd shapes but are meant to be assembled." I looked back at Kathleen to reassure her. "I think I've included some of those tender moments. As I narrow things down, I'd love to run the manuscript by all of you. I won't write anything you don't feel comfortable with."

"We shouldn't dictate what you say," Peg spoke out.

"Thanks, Peg. I won't delete anything that I feel is necessary and true."

THE NEXT DAY I RAN off a hundred and fifty single-spaced pages of what I called my first draft. My most meaningful dreams with all the intricate details slathered the pages of dialogue-less reporting that I saw as strong intention. The historical pieces felt necessary. But they weren't easily fitting into my story line. I was still vacillating about where to begin. The gathered letters from Uncle Martin, Nanny, and her father hung loosely on the framework of my hunt-and-gather project.

"Feedback." I verbalized my next need to Lori, and proudly presented her with a duplicate copy.

"I've already heard most of your dreams. You're always sharing them with me." She emphasized "sharing." "I don't need to be reminded of the heavy experiences from your childhood, Emma."

She placed my work on the floor, beside the reclining chair that supported her as she returned her attention to a *Seinfeld* rerun. I retreated to my office and began a page–by-page re-evaluation. Kathleen was right. Those positive childhood moments weren't prominent enough. It wasn't because we hadn't had them.

In my need to find my emotional "hooks," I hadn't written about the holiday singalongs where Kathleen played for hours so we could get through every verse of every song in her Rodgers and Hammerstein collection. No details had been shared about the myriad dresses Mom carefully cut and sewed for every school dance, or the clever and elaborate costumes she toiled over for every dance recital. Car trips had been left out – the ones on which Dad had taught us to sing the three parts of *Dona Nobis Pacem*. Indeed, the beautiful moments had been there. As sisters we all shared in these treasured parts of our past.

I dug back into the old corrugated box to find one of my favorite pictures of my parents dancing together in a performance when I was about five years old. My father had drawn a thin moustache above his upper lip with a dark-brown eyebrow pencil. They both wore black Spanish costumes with red cummerbunds and tulle ruffles. My mother held a pair of castanets that she knew how to play. Her smile was so authentic I was stunned to see it. Throughout our lives, whenever the opportunity arose they danced together. Everyone enjoyed watching the intimate graceful connection that carried them across the floor as one.

"I want to remember you like this." I spoke to their images as if they were alive. "Help me to hold this memory of you both, dancing your dance as a couple who deeply loved each other."

CHAPTER 38
The Sacred Circle

"Need a hand?" Gina called from the balcony. Peg had already reached the bottom of the stairs. Kathleen and I pulled tote bags, suitcases, and groceries from the car, handing over some and carrying the rest to the suite at the far end of the second floor.

"This was a great idea you had," Peg enthused as she wrapped her arms around Kathleen and pulled her close. "Welcome to our first-ever Sisters' Weekend! I picked up fliers at the front desk." She was waving them in the air. "There's a pool and sauna in the brick building, some interesting dinner and shopping options close by, and if you look between those two buildings," she lowered her voice like she was revealing a deep secret, "you can see the ocean."

"I heard we're expecting rain tomorrow," Gina reported over her shoulder as she tucked her suitcase farther into the corner of the living room, beside the pull-out couch.

"Who's ready for a drink?" Kathleen was holding up a bottle of gin in one hand, tonic in the other.

"I made sure there was ice." Peg was already unpacking her assortment of games and placing them on the coffee table.

"I brought my deviled eggs." Gina handed them to me as we started stocking the refrigerator with our home-made specialties.

Like the inner workings of a clock, we connected and moved each other along, ticking away smoothly and effortlessly in our process of settling in.

After I gave the mixed greens one final toss and we all took our seats, I couldn't resist the delicious opportunity to gaze around the table and savor each word and smile. Two of us had recently hit the fifty-year mark, and here we sat, ready to share three spontaneous days as "the sisterhood." Alongside the roasted chicken and pasta salad, our many blessings sat before us, like sweet condiments.

After we cleared the table, Gina brought out an assortment of treats she had packed and Peg set out the dominoes. It had been a long work week, but we forged ahead on our last ounces of energy. As we finished our second game, Kathleen lifted her reading glasses and rubbed her eyes.

"Time to call it a night," we responded in unprompted unison.

When Gina stepped out of the bathroom in her nightgown and a freshly scrubbed face, without a word she walked past me and lifted the cushions from the pull-out couch. Kathleen raced to assist her before I realized we hadn't discussed sleeping arrangements. They slipped into the fold-out bed, side by side.

"Whenever I sleep at your house, Emma," Gina's voice was playful, "I can't stop dreaming." She turned her head toward our remaining sister and raised her eyebrows. "You can sleep with her, Peg."

"You *never* stop dreaming," I teased. "You just *remember* more of them when you stay with me."

Kathleen lowered her gaze to her latest paperback. "Gina can sleep with the light on," she explained. "I won't bother her."

I knew I could easily rock the family boat with my deeper conversations. On Gina's occasional stays, we had discussed it. But I could also say, with confidence, that when she chose to look into her nightly messages, the dream game had brought her some constructive

214

direction. I had no problem taking responsibility for being the sister who opened the dream gates just by being present. The teasing kept our communication lines open. If Gina and Kathleen believed that manipulated sleeping arrangements could stop their dreaming, I wasn't going to suggest otherwise. I turned and followed Peg into the adjoining bedroom.

IN THE MORNING WE PAIRED up under two umbrellas and romped through puddles. Licorice ropes and malted milk balls passed from hand to hand, reminding us of the penny-candy store that used to stand on the corner, across from our house. Drenched and full, we finally returned to hunker down under the stormy afternoon.

"What kind of tea would you like?" I held up three boxes over four fresh mugs.

Gale-force winds sprayed rain across the picture window, transforming our partial ocean view into an abstract wash, cleansing our palettes for the next course. We gathered around the coffee table to discuss the latest concerns about Dad.

"He's just been diagnosed with leukemia." Kathleen placed the announcement before us like a crucial card that might change the game. "Gina got the call on Thursday. The doctors have suggested transfusions every few days. We need to decide what to do."

"If they can lengthen his life, I think we should give the okay," Peg jumped right in.

Gina reluctantly gave her approval.

My stomach tightened as I thought about my father's raging exit from his dentist's office, angry confusion over where Doug and Peg were taking him in the car, and his inability to remember anything two minutes after it was explained to him. "Dad has signed a living will, hasn't he?" I asked. "Doesn't it say that he not be resuscitated or assisted in the event of a heart attack or his inability to take in food?"

My sisters nodded.

"So, I'm wondering how these ongoing transfusions would be different. Dad doesn't even know us. Sometimes he yells at Margaret until she has to leave, then he climbs into the wrong bed. When they take him out for a doctor's appointment or a medical test, he doesn't know who people are, where he's going, or why. Transfusions could extend this cruel process for a long time."

The heartbreaking circumstances stood before us, waiting for our consideration, as our eighty-five-year-old father hovered between life and death.

"I know leukemia has an emotional charge for us," I continued, "because this is how Eddy died. We're reacting partly to that, but to me it's a sign, a blessing. This disease is shutting down Dad's immune system so his physical body will stop functioning and his spirit can be let go. I'd like to let him pass when he's ready, without any interference – except to alleviate his physical pain. This is what 'comfort measures' mean to me."

"Analise did a reading for me last week." Kathleen's voice was softer than mine. "She looked at Dad's chart to see if he's nearing his time of transition. She doesn't know why Dad's still here."

Peg leaned forward as if we weren't close enough to hear what she was about to say. "Last week at a womens retreat the minister gave us a parable to contemplate. It was long and I wasn't sure I could find anything to comment on, but a few words in the middle of the page jumped out at me: *I am with you for a short while.* After I read it, I felt very strongly and told the group, 'I have to go see my father.'"

Her arms opened to the linking chain of hands that pulled us to the center of the room where we tightly drew each other in and Peg's tears poured into our love.

"When you see him," I turned to her, "even if you don't think he can hear you, tell him everything you need to say, Peg. Tell him how much you love him and that it's okay to go."

"That's what I was wondering. Should I talk to him?"

"He needs to hear from you. Even if he seems incoherent, you can speak to him, and he'll hear you. If you pray to him, he'll hear you. His spirit won't leave until he's ready to go."

"I never told her I loved her," Gina burst out. "I never told Mom that I loved her."

We were back at the piercing moment of our mother's death, with the burden of denial and carefully orchestrated lack of disclosure that had left all of us with no time to say what we needed to say. It sat heavily on us as we held ourselves open to our deepest vulnerabilities. We moved in as close as our bodies would allow; each turning our head to rest on a shoulder beside us.

Kathleen's eyes met Gina's. The circle opened. "Mom told me, when you were born, she was so happy to have another little girl." The voice of the eldest spoke a truth none of us had known. "She loved you very much, Gina."

The four of us remained open to the tears that still needed releasing, the feelings that might still need expression, until Kathleen stepped in with the final question: "Peg," If Dad passed before you were able to get there, would you be okay with it?"

She didn't hesitate, "I think I would."

We all looked to Gina.

"I'd be okay."

We went on, through the following hours, with a renewed appreciation of our delicate and cherished relationship. It was hard to leave those two behind for two additional days, but the next morning Kathleen and I had to get home, and back to work. Peg called before the next day was done.

"Can you hear me all right?" she asked in her demonstrative voice. "I'm calling from my cell phone."

"Yes, perfectly, what's up?"

"Gina just called the convalescent home. Dad passed away last night."

She waited for my response. I couldn't speak.

"Emma, I walked on the beach yesterday and I prayed. I talked to God and then to Dad. I said everything I needed to say, and that it was all right with me if this was his time to go."

Our phone chain could hardly find words to express the astonishing power of our sacred weekend. We felt as connected to our father in his transition as we had when three of us sensed our mother's visitation on the night of her death. Such an immediate response to Peg's prayers was an undeniable confirmation. When Nanny had returned to our Granville homestead and quietly passed over, she had taught the first of these great lessons about the gentle and perfect nature of dying. The beauty in death is as rich as a birth when witnessed in the fullness of truth and acceptance.

Now, the opportunity stood before us to embark upon the journey of closure – to say goodbye to our father in a way that twenty years ago, with our mother, we had been unable to do.

CHAPTER 39
Saying Goodbye

I missed Lori's fingers tapping on the back of my hand as we accelerated at full throttle. Peg was erasing and penciling in a different answer to her crossword puzzle. Kathleen had cast a row of pink stitches onto a knitting needle, the beginnings of a blanket for her first granddaughter, due in a few months. Opaque clouds blanketed our windows, causing me to ponder how it must feel to be piloting a plane filled with passengers when you can't see anything but white vapor in front of you. Through closed eyes, I envisioned us coming out safely on the other side; and in the imagined sunlight I began to contemplate how the four of us were going to pull off Margaret's last-minute request.

"Left high and dry," my father would have said when the minister unexpectedly left town, dropping his entire responsibility in our lap. What else could we do? Directing the service meant inventing it. In the past twenty-four hours, my willingness had faded.

"There she is," Peg pointed toward the hand that waved over the heads of a dark-haired family that was also drifting toward us from a distant corner of the Orlando airport. In this relieved moment that only the fourth sister could activate, Peg began waving back, as Kathleen checked to be sure she had everything. I pulled a fresh water bottle from my carry-on bag and rushed along to keep up.

"How was your flight?" I asked, as Gina ran into my hug.

"Great! Everything was on time, and the weather was so clear."

"The rental cars are this way," Peg was directing from a few feet ahead of us. Kathleen was attempting to unfold and read her carefully organized list of our appointed responsibilities.

Beneath the rhythm of our accelerated heartbeats, there were words that needed to be said, and questions were waiting behind feelings that wanted to be felt, but we had to get to the bank before four and check into the hotel before dinner with Margaret. As Kathleen and Gina finished placing their bags in the trunk, I slid into the front seat with Peg, who was already inserting the key into the ignition.

The heat of the mid-day sun penetrated our windows as we headed from Orlando to Lake Placid. Peg turned on the air conditioning, and we stopped talking about plane trips and baggage pickups. Errands we would eventually attend to fell to the back of our minds. Silence embraced us as we began to settle.

"When I was in my first semester at Northfield," Kathleen reported from the back seat, after a long stretch of our conversationless drive. "I wrote home because I needed some money for shampoo and soap. A few dollars for some essentials."

I turned to Peg, who kept her eyes on the road, then I twisted around to half-face Kathleen.

"Shampoo and soap," Kathleen repeated in an exceptionally clear way, as if she were restating the facts in order to be sure she was recording them accurately on her list. "I waited a week for Dad's reply. He sent me Monopoly money."

"As a joke?" Gina asked.

"It wasn't a joke," Kathleen assured her.

"At least he paid for your education, Kathleen." I jumped right in. "When I was in Springfield and asked for money to pay my rent, he insisted he couldn't help me." The essential steeping of the bitter herbs had begun.

In the distance, an electrical pole seemed to pierce the earth and my awareness like a spear, flinging its wires into infinity. Perched on one of them, a hawk stood facing us, as still as the humid air.

The messenger, I thought, quoting the Medicine Cards. The hawk was reminding me to look at things from a higher perspective, beyond these emotional pains.

THE SMELL OF MOLD IN our adjoining motel rooms was so strong we insisted on moving to the second floor. I wouldn't dare tell my sisters I felt we had attracted this toxic situation because of the old energies we were releasing; but when our physical move to a higher level brought us a cleaner and fresher space, it seemed we had made an important shift.

Gina was placing the finishing touches of frosty pink on her lips when Peg and Kathleen stepped in to move us along. "We're due at Margaret's." Peg pointed to her watch.

"If we can take just a second," I sat on the bed, "I found something in my bottom drawer last week that I've saved since our wedding. A tape of our ceremony. Someone must have stood on the balcony to record it. You can barely hear our vows being made at the altar, but Dad came through, crystal clear." I felt my emotions rising. "I had copies made for each of you and for Margaret. I thought his singing might be an appropriate addition to his service."

At the villa we all stood around Dad's CD player, as still as bare trees, waiting for the organist's opening notes, holding our breaths in anticipation of the inevitable "Our Father."

When had we last heard him sing?

The powerful tenor voice that had been silent for over twenty-five years rang out, rushing into the places where we had been tightly holding on. His physical presence touched us as our hearts opened to our father's words, but the reality of his absence returned as we exited the front door. From now on, each threshold step would be in his memory.

WHEN WE RETURNED TO OUR motel rooms, Peg set *The Bible* and *The Prophet* at the center of her bed. "I've marked a few passages," she said to us, "but they need your approval. I'm fine with reading whatever you choose." She lifted a highlighted curl from in front of her face and wrapped it behind her ear. Community theater productions had made her comfortable with public speaking.

"I'd like to read you my eulogy, to see if I've left anything out," I added.

"I think I'd be okay with reading something, if it isn't too long," Gina sat on Peg's bed and was warming up to the progression of things.

Kathleen didn't mention the music she had packed at the bottom of her suitcase. She stood in the doorway between the room Gina and I were staying in and the one she was sharing with Peg, comfortably poised, outside the arena for dreaming up a funeral service. As she watched us begin our collective review she peeled the protective paper from a hotel glass.

"Margaret would like to include the Twenty-Third Psalm." Peg was on a roll. "We can all read it together. The funeral home must have a copier. We'll get that all straightened out in the morning. The service isn't until two. We'll have plenty of time."

When I read my eulogy, no one requested a change. It seemed I hadn't forgotten anything. The service was complete.

"Anyone for a nite-cap?' Kathleen asked.

"I'd like one!" Gina was pulling a tiny memo pad from her purse and flipping through five pages of notes. "I had a dream."

"Oh no!" Kathleen's blatant reaction was unlike her.

"I could really use some help with this one." Gina sheepishly looked to me.

We've come a long way from a week ago, I was thinking, *when Gina didn't want to sleep in the same room with me, fearing that I might cause her to dream.*

As if Kathleen hadn't initially resisted, she offered to begin the game. Leaning on her elbows, she playfully threw out suggestions about what Gina's dream might mean, if it were her own. Peg's attraction to puzzles placed her next in line, and by the time I threw in my observations, Gina was sure it was time to address some problems with her supervisor at work. If she didn't, her situation would become wilder and more distressing, as her dream had clearly pointed out.

One by one, we separated from the group, slipped into our nightgowns, and returned to say goodnight. "Sweet dreams," I called to the others when we had all tucked in.

"No way!" Kathleen had jumped out of bed and was standing in the doorway again. "I don't want to dream!" She was running a flattened hand across her throat like the blade of a knife. I lifted myself up to show her I was listening to her complaint. "Mine are all nightmares, Emma. Everyone in them is headless. I'm not interested."

Tonight, I didn't have the energy to continue a conversation with anyone who resisted the dreaming process. None of us had the capacity for another drop of discussion. As Kathleen backed away and returned to her bed, I placed my hands over my heart, feeling the heat I was generating. A connecting light penetrated the thin wall between us and surrounded Kathleen as we drifted off to sleep.

CHOKING, I WOKE UP THINKING, *she's choking.* The sounds from the next room sent me straight through the darkness like an arrow to a memorized target. To my astonishment, Kathleen was standing between the beds. It was Peg who held up her hands, frozen in unconscious surrender.

"It's okay," she called out to Gina, who ran to the end of her bed. "It wasn't a bad dream. I was walking toward a closet, and when I reached for the door, it swung open on its own. It startled me. The closet was filled with bright light. I wasn't afraid, just startled."

The sight of us huddled around Peg provoked relieved laughter. No interpretations of her powerful and effortless opening needed to be exchanged. She had dreamed the dream for all of us, as we were cautiously opening our own closet doors.

IN THE MORNING WE DRESSED and went to the funeral home to make our last minute preparations for the afternoon service we were still creating. The chapel in the front room of our childhood home had been a palace in comparison to this old space. With thread-bare carpeting and dark paneled walls, it felt more like an Elks lodge than a funeral home. I imagined Dad would have felt right at home at an Elks lodge. He would have been fine with his ashes in the white marble box placed at the center of the wooden folding table we were doing our best to transform into an altar with a linen table runner and assorted mementos we were pulling from plastic bags. Kathleen had stepped away from the creative process and moved to the back of the room where she sat on the wooden bench in front of an electric organ that looked like it might be old enough to have stopped working altogether.

"I love this picture." Gina was holding up the framed photograph for Peg and me to admire. "This is the way I want to remember him." She pulled it toward her, running her index finger along the bright smile that reflected the fullness of Dad's spirit. Smoke spiraled from his cigar to his sparkling gray eyes.

"This is only half of the ashes," Peg turned to me and pointed to the marble box. "The rest are going home with us."

"You're kidding. I never heard of such a thing."

"I guess they do it all the time. We'll bury them next to Mom."

"I think I'd like to play a hymn." Kathleen broke in. "Could we choose it over lunch?"

ON OUR WAY TO THE restaurant, we continued to consider the words of songs and how many verses we should sing, but our minds were on overload. Fatigue had caught up with all of us, causing a wave of giggles. "We're getting a little punchy," Kathleen felt obliged to interject. "I need some caffeine. A double iced tea, no ice."

"I remember this place. Dad and Margaret came here often." Gina was looking for their favorite booth. *The perfect location to make our last-minute decisions.*

When we finished our meal, Gina motioned for the check. Our waitress was already on her way to the table, pitcher in hand. She raised it to my glass and looked directly into my eyes.

"How ya doin' on tea?"

"How did you know I was an Auntie?" I sat dumbfounded at the words that I just spoke. No one in my family ever called me "Auntie!" My astonished expression sparked an outburst of irrepressible laughter from all four of us.

"It's a personal joke," Gina was explaining to our flustered waitress as she took the check from her. "On tea... Auntie..." she attempted to interpret the missed pun. Tears were rolling from our eyes.

No matter how ridiculous it sometimes sounded, Dad never passed up the opportunity to respond with a play on words. "Oops, I peed on the table," he would chuckle, when a green pea rolled off his plate. He had a list of fictitious books he could rattle off the names of, at any moment, like *Little Yellow Waterfall* by I. P. Standing. He found great joy in playing with words in this way, and I was the daughter who probably judged him the most when he blurted out such corny and embarrassing comments. I never would have thought to respond to the unsuspecting waitress in this way. It made perfect sense that his telltale remark would be channeled through me. We could not misinterpret our father's bittersweet presence.

A FEW CARS HAD ALREADY pulled into the parking lot by the time we returned to the funeral home. We took each other's hands and entered the darkened room, made our way down the central aisle of folding chairs, and sat in the front row alongside Margaret and Seth. I imagined my father's spirit floating above the marble box and smiling over us. Noises at the entrance subsided. Fewer than twenty elderly friends had taken their seats. I stood and stepped behind the podium.

"When we were all very young, my three sisters and I often gathered in our basement, to perform for our family. Dressed in velvet jackets, tutus, and scarves pulled from an attic trunk, we sang, danced, and felt the love of our family. We are deeply connected to those memories as we find ourselves collaborating once again, this time, to say our final farewells to our father." From here, we simply flowed, as we always had, handing responsibilities off to each other in our final ceremony to celebrate our father's life. I spoke about how his beautiful tenor voice had become the fabric of our being, how music, theater, and dance had become integrated parts of our lives. I remarked that his deepest intention had always been to do the right thing, and I know that regardless of any indiscriminate choices, this is what he truly believed in.

I headed for the sound system at the back of the room as Peg prepared the group for our father's rendidion of *The Lord's Prayer*. In closing, we played a recording of the *Benediction* sung by the Northfield Alumni Choir which included Kathleen and Gina. From the front of the room, Gina positioned the tape she had tucked away in her carry-on bag for this moment.

ONLY SIX OF US STOOD at the tall white crypt surrounded by palm trees and flooded with light. Seth dropped his mother's arm to lift Dad's ashes into place. Kathleen had already begun the hand-to-hand linking of sisters when we joined our voices in the gentle harmonies of *Dona Nobis Pacem.*

"Your father taught you to sing that?" Margaret asked with tears in her eyes. She had never heard us sing.

Rest in peace. My mind spoke to the brass plaque marking the niche that holds his remains. I knew he would.

My head dropped as I walked in the cool shade that led us back to the cars. A large reddish feather with narrow stripes lay directly on my path. I lifted it from the grass, wondering how I might pack it to bring it safely home. My hand gently slid over its smooth shimmer before I held it up to Seth.

"A hawk," he confirmed.

"Are you sure?" my amazement forced me to question.

"I'm sure, Emma. This feather is from a red-tailed hawk."

IT ALL FELT LIKE A dream. A fleeting, memorable dream that left us with a hazy memory of how we had said our goodbyes. We returned to the airport with lighter hearts and a box of ashes Peg was carrying back to Massachusetts.

"I'm going to pay more attention to my dreams," Kathleen said, leaning over her knitting and speaking clearly into my ear, once we had leveled off and were soaring homeward.

I smiled.

"I'll try what you suggested, Emma, and ask before I go to sleep that whatever needs to be shown will come, in more gentle ways – ways I can understand and accept."

CHAPTER 40

New Dreams

"Aunt Emma!" Shari called from the upstairs window. "We're about to begin the tour." My niece's yard was bustling with new friends and our expanding family. A variety of tables had been set out on her lawn, with matching tablecloths. Kathleen was combining and rearranging Shari's nearly devoured signature appetizers, to make room for the entrees that were waiting to come out from the kitchen. I pulled the pink azalea from the back seat. Lori lifted her homemade guacamole and my pasta salad from the trunk. We exchanged nods and waved to the familiar guests as we made our way to the back door.

"Welcome!" Shari was summoning us to join the others who patiently waited in the front hall. "You're just in time." Her steps were slow under the extra weight. Like a mother goose leading her flock, she waddled up the wooden staircase, routing us down the freshly painted hallway and into the baby's room. "It's nearly finished," she chirped, rolling her eyes in acknowledgment of the work it had taken to get here.

The awareness came upon me like an unexpected flower that has popped up across the yard and stands as tall as the plant from which it has sprung. Both of Kathleen's children were now married, had bought homes, and were starting families. It seemed I was just picking them up and holding them in my arms.

I followed the group down the stairs and out the back entrance, then glanced across the lawn. Kathleen was taking her first break of the day, carefully choosing each food item as she made every effort to stay with a low-point Weight Watchers lunch. I sneaked up behind her and wrapped my arm around her tiny waist.

"Hey." She planted a kiss on my cheek. "Did you have a hard time finding us?"

"Not at all. We got a late start. The drive actually turned out to be shorter than I expected. What a beautiful old house!"

With so much happening for a grandmother, one would think my sister's next words would follow this vein of thought, but as we took our seats at the shaded table near the rope swing that had been left by the previous owners, Kathleen was ready to spill something more personal.

"I have to tell you, Emma..." her voice trailed off as she held up her glass and nodded to Gina, letting her know she had found the iced tea. "I've been dreaming!"

The deviled egg slipped out of my hand and landed topside down on my plate. I was smiling so hard my eyes were tearing.

"And everyone has heads!" she crowed.

Eye to eye, we giggled like the little sisters who long ago tiptoed around the dining room table together, ready to revisit the trunk of magical costumes. "As soon as I asked for gentler messages," she looked to see that no one else was close enough to hear, "the headless nightmares stopped."

I turned the egg over, once again lifting it to my lips, savoring the flavor and texture of the processed yolk. *When we gently process our core issues,* my mind couldn't help interpreting, *this satisfying softness inevitably appears.*

MY OWN PROCESS CONTINUED TO make itself known. I bought a new computer and converted all my writings. With the insertion of paper and the push of a button, my second draft released into my hands. Sections I was reluctant to express honestly were choppy and short, haphazardly inserted between the more positive dreams and insights. A drive beyond expression kept me typing away, day into night.

Images of unique quilts returned to my dreams, where I continued to turn the multifaceted three-dimensional pieces in every direction in an attempt to fit them together. I wasn't sure, in the dreams, how my quilt was going to come out, but I remained inspired.

CHAPTER 41

The Bear And The Hawk

A *huge mother bear is standing upright on the horizon,* I had
written in my journal. *I'm petrified of her. She senses her baby
has been in my house and I'm afraid she's going to break in and tear the
place apart. I'm locking the windows, knowing she could easily break
through them.*

*The larger-than-life grizzly is hovering in the distance, ready to
advance.* My mind replayed the dream as I looked through the
windshield at the interstate highway before me. *Why am I so afraid
of this bear, the Native Americans' most powerful symbol of healing?
Why can't I just open the windows and release my fear?*

The cars up ahead began to stop, one by one, backing up toward
me like an approaching mud slide, determined to impede my forward
motion. I was grateful I had started early as I glided to a halt and
glanced at the long lines ahead of me. *I don't think I have a map in
the glove compartment.* I slipped into the breakdown lane and eased
toward the next exit, behind other travelers who were willing to take
an alternate route.

My windows subtly rattled as I pulled in to the gas station
and faced a tightly closed, two-car bay. The heavy-metal music
blaring from an old radio seemed to focus the mechanic who stood
hunched over the engine of a car with a dented hood. I stepped into
the adjoining room where soda and snack machines were barely

accessible behind a new shipment of cardboard boxes. The young man behind the register seemed to be perfectly comfortable in the midst of it all.

"You're not too far out," he reassured, as he jotted down directions on the back of a discarded receipt. "This'll be a nice scenic route for ya. Where ya goin'?"

"A dream workshop," I said, pointing at the Mounds bar to his left.

"That's a big thing now," he confidently reported back.

"Really?" I leaned in, encouraging more.

"Yeah, I heard it on the radio last week. People are gettin' together and talkin' about 'em."

"Dreams are very important," I said, taking hold of the candy bar and handing him a five-dollar bill. "They come to guide us through the challenges in our lives."

"Like finding your way to Lenox?" He laughed.

"Like finding my way to Lenox."

TWELVE YEARS STOOD BETWEEN THE uncovering of my wounded soul on the massage table, my inner child crying for her mother and my return to Kripalu. Over those years the retreat center had transformed as much as I had. No longer an ashram reserved for yoga and meditation, Kripalu was now a renowned healing center that offered diversified programs and spiritual studies as the Center for Yoga and Health.

I was here for a three-day intensive workshop with Robert Moss, a teacher I had found on-line. To my amazement, he had recently opened a dream school in Connecticut. Over the past year I had made many trips to his monthly meetings, eager to participate in playfully informal dream theater and to practice dream re-entry. I appreciated every opportunity to close my eyes, clear my mind, and journey with the dream group. I had found it remarkably effortless to notice feelings and sensations, and to trust them. My very first dream re-entry experience remains a powerful teaching. It unfolded during my second class at the dream school.

The sounds of rattles and drums filled our gathering room. I opened my pulsing palms wider to the circle of souls who held clear intention and a sense of adventure.

"A dream is a place," Robert explained, as we quieted to his teaching. "If you give a clear enough description, you can lead others back into your dreamscape, and together you can search for answers to lingering questions."

Really? My mind stretched out the word like warm molasses.

"So, find a partner and decide who would like to go first," Robert directed. "As the dreamer, share the dream you would like to know more about, and choose a place, within the dream, where you and your partner will meet. You have a few minutes to do this."

I turned to Beth, who was also new to the concept of re-entering dreams, and was relieved when she asked me to share my dream first. In this initiatory stage I didn't feel very confident that I could bring back any meaningful information for someone else.

"I had this dream quite a long time ago," I told her. "I was walking down a set of dark wooden stairs and at the bottom, behind a curtain, was a male presence. I was so scared I tried to scream, but I couldn't. I want to know why I'm so afraid of that presence," I explained, so we could seek out that specific answer when we re-entered together. Then I went on to describe our entry point: "The walls along the staircase, in my dream, are also dark wood. The floor-to-ceiling window is on the left, at the bottom of the stairs, on the ground floor. It's covered with a beige curtain that's billowing. Is that enough information for you to see it in your mind?" I asked.

After she nodded I went on. "I guess we'll meet each other there," I half smiled, raising my eyebrows at the thought of it. We covered our eyes with colorful bandanas and lay back with the others like the spokes of a wheel.

"All right…" Robert's familiar introduction to getting down to business nudged us along. He lifted his round flat drum by the crossed wooden pieces in the back that reinforced the large rim. I finished wiggling into position as he invited us to "let the drumming lead the way."

Breathing into the monotone rhythm, I sensed myself at the foot of the stairs. Although my closed eyes peered into darkness, I could sense what I was doing. *Where's Beth?* My inner voice whined, trying hard to focus on the course of action we were supposed to be taking. *Should I actually see Beth beside me?* I wondered, while the beat of the drum, deliberate as a metronome, ticked away our precious time. *This experiment isn't working,* I inwardly complained under the dimmed overhead lights.

The seemingly endless span of time, I suppose, was only a few minutes before my inner commentary ceased. I relaxed into my deepening breath and gave up pushing. *It wouldn't be the end of the world to come back without answers,* I had decided.

It was at this moment, when I gave up pushing, that my eyelids began to flutter. I recognized this as the activation of a deeper process. The staircase appeared, then the window with the long beige drape. I shot through the curtain, feet first, and flew through a dark tunnel. I could feel the speed and then the sudden stop.

The warm glow of a ritual fire outlined the silhouettes of indigenous people gathered around me. I was lying on a healing table, and I could clearly distinguish the feathered headdress and painted face of a Native American medicine man standing at my feet. I was stunned at the clarity of this vision I had found myself in, and the comfort I felt in this setting.

I knew my stomach was contracting, although I didn't feel the sensation of it. I was attempting to give birth, but there was a block. The healer stepped to my side and lifted a sharp instrument that reflected the flames of the fire. Aware of myself also lying in the circle of dreamers I felt my eyes flutter again. *Reversing the blade in his hand, the man leaned over me and skillfully inserted it into the far side of my belly. I felt no pain as he pulled it back across. I was focused on the way in which he was cutting, with focused precision. His large brown hands reached into my open incision, lifting the child from my womb and holding it above my head in one hand, severing the umbilical cord with the knife he held in the other. There was a shrill cry.*

Inside my journey I was reaching for my baby, opening my hands wide, but the medicine man held him beyond my grasp. The witnesses moved in closer.

Why am I being kept from my son? I silently questioned.

The moist maroon lining of my wide-open belly was drying up. It peeled away to expose the white bones of my skeleton. Fearless and free of pain, I strained to hear what the elders were saying to each other. They were making an important decision.

My spirit rose from the disintegrating body that lay on the table, and in a ghost-like form it rushed into the baby's body. Now I was observing from above as the external shell of my physical self broke apart and fell away in paper-thin pieces that floated to the ground like a pile of dry November leaves. A vital energy connected me to the innocent purity of the infant, my new form.

The drumbeat quickened. Awareness of physical reality returned to our circle. I rolled to my side and wrapped my arms around my knees to integrate the journey and take it all in before sitting up to face Beth.

"I'm not sure." She seemed disappointed in her report. "I don't think I can help you very much, Emma."

With Robert's reminder not to edit any of what we recalled, she took another moment to reflect upon her notes.

"It seems silly. I just got rhyming words, like...precision."

She shrugged, opening her empty hands. I nodded for her to continue.

"Incision," she added. "Decision."

Beth and I were completely aligned to share the magic we had come to the dream school to own. When my dream journey shifted from the draped window to a sacred ritual, I understood I was being given something powerfully transforming: ancestral assistance in letting go of my old self that held old beliefs. I had given birth to the new male part of myself.

Sitting on the bed in the private room I had reserved at Kripalu, I thought about the Native American energy that ran to my assistance at the very moment I joined the dream school family. Today, this workshop was calling me toward healing again, by a grizzly bear and another deep fear.

After dinner and our opening dream circle I tucked into bed, singing the words we had repeated as we closed, "Healer of All, come Blessed One." At ten of four I woke without recalling anything. *"Bummer!" I really wanted something juicy to work with in the days ahead.* I knew that if we take a moment and curl up in the way we were sleeping, a tiny fragment might spark a memory. Feeling the pressure in my full bladder, I closed my eyes and opened my mind.

I could hear the faint knock at the door. Someone had been provided access. *Yes.* My dream was flooding into conscious awareness.

THE VISITATION

I'm sitting in a small cabin where two men have died and come back to me. One is my father but I don't see him. There's a knock at the door. A young Native American man enters and acknowledges that he is my brother. I can't get over how alive the departed spirit looks.

"I've brought you three gifts," he says.

The scene changes and I'm upstairs in a house filled with friends of these two deceased men, my father and my brother. I hear Gina's voice coming up the stairs, but no one here knows her. Taking her hand, I guide her to a small table in the corner.

"I'm surprised to see you, Gina."

"How are you doing," she asks, "this night of funerals?"

"You wouldn't believe it," I tell her. "I've never seen people who have died before, an elder and his son. It was as if they were both alive. I was honored, deeply honored."

Have we been father, son, and daughter in a past life? I questioned. Are we so connected that there's a karmic reason my father had to experience the loss of Eddy after such a short time? Somehow, Gina understands.

My attention shifted to my full bladder, but my dream vision pulled me back. I returned to the chair in the cabin, at my Native American brother's side, in a tandem dream re-entry.

"What do you want to know?" he asks.

"More about the three gifts."

The white buffalo-skin medicine pouch dangling from his hand is plain, except for a small medallion on the left side, embellished with aqua beads and small feathers. On the right is the long thin feather of a red-tailed hawk, like the one I found in Florida, the day of my father's funeral.

"This feather holds a message for you," my brother explains.

He brings the second gift forward, a long rectangular buckskin pouch with rawhide straps hanging from it. As I carefully take it from him, it falls open. I pull out a beautiful peace pipe.

"You must come to a peaceful place with us," he says. "You must smoke the pipe to honor and let us go."

Tears glide along the rims of my closed eyes. Have I psychically been holding onto him by carrying the pain of my brother's loss for all these years?

"Now we go to the third gift." My brother glances at a small oval pouch at my feet. When I pick it up, my fingers squeeze the soft leather. The razor sharpness of what's inside forces me to release my curious grip.

When I reach in, the fit is perfect. I remove the bear paw. It's the size of my own hand and it has long, sharp claws. "This is your power," he explains. "Take it. Hold it. Place it between your hands."

Once again, I'm crying.

As I physically place my hands together, a burst of heat and charged energy radiates through them. "What is your name?" I ask, as I hold the bear paw to my heart.

"Howling Wind," he replies, "I've been coming to you for a long time and you've been noticing me. Whenever you hear the wind howling, you will know I am with you. Go inward and ask for me. I am your spirit guide and will assist you in the difficult times."

WITH KNEES PRESSED TOGETHER, I shuffled toward the bathroom to honor my physical needs. I passed the door of a room across the hall, then stopped and turned around. The cold November winds howled behind it.

"Thank you, my brother, my spirit guide, Howling Wind," I said softly. Intense energy filled me, and his message returned: *Remember the peace pipe.*

WITH ALL SPIRITUAL WORKSHOPS, THERE is a quickening as the days unfold. I continued to deepen my trust in stepping in and out of the dream world. As Robert would say, I was becoming a "frequent flier" on the spiritual airways as I integrated all the gifts given. On our final afternoon he offered up the space to take a private journey to the dream that still needed more clarity. I lay back, placing my purple bandana over my eyes as the lights dimmed. The heartbeat pulse of the drumming carried me:

> *...to the outside of the cabin where I first met Howling Wind.*
>
> *A red-tailed hawk flies toward me, landing on my wrist with a strength that calls for immediate respect. I can feel his sharp talons wrapped around my forearm so physically that it's hard to determine if he hasn't actually flown through our classroom door and locked himself around my flesh and bone. We are staring into each other's eyes. We recognize the souls behind them. I refuse to blink, fearing that even the most delicate closing and reopening might disconnect us.*
>
> *His wings open, and he lifts me up, out of the room, into the sky, to heights I could never have imagined reaching. When I think we can't go any higher, he releases me, and suddenly I'm flying beside him. His keen sense of vision draws his eyes to the ground, and immediately I can see what he sees. My bone structure is transforming. I can feel my own powerful wings lifting my body slightly with every vigorous down stroke. I'm sensing the air currents as I maneuver through them. Climbing*

*higher and higher, I clearly see what is miles below. I have
become the hawk.*

*My head drops and I'm diving straight down, confident in
my ability to land. My wings open wide, pressing into the air
as my claws extend to grip the open-armed branch.*

The sensation of using my own power filled my body. I was now
prepared for flights that would carry me safely into the mystery
ahead. The drumming called me back almost beyond words. Robert
was at my side.

"The red-tailed hawk," I whispered.

"Yes," he replied calmly. "I saw him."

CHAPTER 42

Spirits At Rest

The broken asphalt path, scarcely wide enough, led us, car by car, past the elaborate headstones that clearly marked where prominent families had been buried. Thin deteriorating slabs that stood, barely visible or legible, seemed to be whispering *I once had life and spirit, too.*

As children we had gathered here every Memorial Day, Brownies and Girl Scouts wearing banners and badges, eager to march between the firetrucks and cadenced bands, waving to cheering bystanders. As we grew older, we rarely visited the Granville Cemetery, where a grove of verdant trees protected the back corner that now drew us closer to our own family's granite headstone. The twelve newly chiseled letters had brought balance and finality. Our father's name now completed the symmetrical list of four beloved souls passed.

Firmly planted in the ground, beside the larger headstone, a modest plaque shimmered in its newness. Engraved with the words "Edward Morgan Jr.," it stood as the replacement of the broken marble pillar Dad had originally set on Eddy's grave, stolen by vandals long ago.

Peg pressed the mahogany urn to her breast like a precious child. Lori and I walked, shoulder to shoulder, feeling each other's gentle support. As we meandered in our silent groups, Shari lifted her daughter, Marissa, from her husband's arms, boosting her higher to lessen the weight. Little Josh sidled up to his mother and let go of his father's hand, as Jonathan thoughtfully walked toward the small hand-dug opening that lay vacant and waiting.

Our circle found its form as Peg held up the smooth container that Doug had carefully turned on his lathe. She passed it to Gina and it continued moving forward, an occasional palm sliding over its cool surface in a final farewell.

Jonathan took his time placing the urn into the deep hole, then he gathered up four items he had brought with him. He revealed the ball marker and the worn metal head of his first putter that had once belonged to his grandfather, before placing them into the ground. Kneeling, he nestled a tiny bottle of scotch and then a six-pack of cigars into the remaining corners. Placing his hands on his knees, he pushed himself into a stand and unfolded the paper with typewritten Scriptures he had also carried with him.

He struggled to hold his emotions back. I could feel them inside of him, trying to break free. I wanted to rush forward and hug the grief from him as he lowered his eyes in a final private prayer.

Unexpectedly, he returned to the earthen hole to remove his last-placed item. He peeled the red cellophane strip from the small box, but it stuck to his dampend fingers, dangling from them until he slid his hand deep into his pocket, to wipe it free. One cigar was all he removed, before closing the lid on the others and returning them to their moist dark corner. "For Pop," he said, striking the match.

As my nephew took the first puff, the aroma of the smoke ascending from his cigar's bright tip drew us back in time, to the dining room table and quiet nights in front of the television. It felt as inviting a fragrance as the lilac blooms that called us into every spring. This gesture, an instinctive opportunity, caused me to reach out my hand. Jonathan eagerly passed it on.

"This is a sacred smoking," I barely whispered, before drawing in and releasing the smoke for Eddy, and for my father. By holding the purest intention, I fulfilled the final responsibility of my brother's dream message:

"You must smoke a peace pipe for your father and me."

Jonathan stepped aside and returned with a square piece of fresh sod. His eyes moistened. "I stopped at Sunset Ridge this morning," he confessed, holding up the tiny section of grass he had cut from the outer edge of the first fairway at the golf course that had been his grandfather's short lived dream-come-true. "The new owners were happy to oblige." He smiled as he filled the hole with dark soil and capped the little grave with his special gift, tucking it in around the edges like a warm blanket.

"A hawk," Jon whispered, his head uplifted.

Kathleen looked to me. "It's been circling for a while."

As I DROVE TOWARD HOME through the clear night, Lori turned to me, holding her thought for quite a long time before passing it on in a lowered voice. "Emma," she paused. "Did you notice at the cemetery, whenever anyone spoke your dad's name, a strong wind blew through the trees?

"Really?" I turned away from the road for just a second to see if she was still staring at me. "The wind?"

"I don't know if anyone else heard it, but it was almost eerie. Every time someone mentioned your dad…"

Stunning, I thought. *From Lori's lips.* I hadn't told her anything about my experiences at Kripalu. A physical encounter with my deceased brother would have been beyond "weird" to her, a Native American brother named "Howling Wind" I believed to be Eddy. She never would have accepted it.

"Thank you," I finally said. "You don't know how much I appreciate your telling me this." Her blonde curls were still shaking off the whole thing. "This is really helpful, Lori. Now, I have absolutely no doubt that spirits are settled."

CHAPTER 43

Not Again

I had run off many drafts, cut out sections, and added new material. "My book's almost done," I hoped, as I handed my latest manuscript to my sisters for their approval. I was starting to tell people I had written a book, and could finally visualize it in print. Although Lori still wasn't interested in reading it, she was quick to ask if I was willing to read it to her when she took her baths at night.

It was actually helpful for me to hear the rhythm of my words as I read them out loud. I noticed where I was rushing and where I still wasn't ready to divulge my deeper truths. I secretly hoped that reading those chapters that described the challenges of our relationship might bring some sort of healing to us, but it didn't even spark a discussion.

Peg called somewhere around that time, when I had finished reading the book to Lori, to let me know that all three sisters had finished reading their manuscripts. We chose a date to meet and go over them together.

"I don't want to hold you back," Kathleen was emphatic when we all sat at Peg's, with copies in hand. "I just need to tell you, your experiences were different from mine."

What felt to me like disapproval caused us all to hold back. No one else spoke as Kathleen took a breath in preparation for her next comment. "I don't agree that Dad was unfaithful," she said with the clear intention she had developed over the years.

I picked at the corners of my copy, then asked Peg straight out, "What do you think? Does it seem to you that Dad might have been involved with the woman who named her son after him?"

"Yes," she said, in her matter-of-fact voice, "it could have happened."

"Gina? What do you think?" I could feel my old prickly energy right out there, pushing for a response to at least one of my lifelong questions.

"The facts were there," the two of them agreed, "It was very possible."

Kathleen let them have their say before returning to our discussion. "Your experiences were different from mine," she calmly repeated, "but go for it. Say what you need and bring your story and your writing into the world. I'm not trying to hold you back. I just need you to know how I feel."

Kathleen wasn't going to become the wobbly foundation that could dismantle the complex project I had invested years in. It wasn't going to be a dispute with one of my sisters that would temporarily send me reeling away from my creative undertaking. What stood waiting to knock me off of my center was the disharmony I thought Lori and I could work out, once the book was finished. My writing was my baby, my healing truth coming forward, my top priority. I was determined to provide a safe delivery.

On a crisp fall morning, my acrylic paints lay before me as I stood on the patio under the back deck, facing the banks of chrysanthemums that brought a sense of hope to a garden slowly dying off. An old, discarded chair had given me another creative project to focus on.

"I'm meeting Pam at Trader Joe's." Lori whisked past me, picking up my jar of red paint and shaking it. She had known Pam in high school. They had recently reconnected at the gym. Lori had signed up for Pam's aerobic class and Pam had come to me for a massage. They had hung out in our garden together, watching the birds on the feeders, talking about their externally different relationships and how they were actually so much the same.

When Lori and I were invited to Pam's anniversary party, Pam and her husband seemed to socialize with the guests more than each other. Lori left me alone much of the night, as she bounced around the room and hung out wherever her reacquainted buddy went.

"What's going on?" I lost it on the way home. "What's going on with Pam?"

Into the morning hours Lori denied any infidelity. There wasn't a word I could say that could provoke anything otherwise. So today, when Lori shook my red paint and told me she was meeting Pam to go grocery shopping, all my questions had already been refuted.

"She doesn't cook much," Lori added, to make their meeting seem more necessary than impulsive. "I'm going to show her how I make some of my easier dishes." With Lori's unbounded interest in food, it was easy for me to slip into the fantasy that she was simply taking her friend grocery shopping. *Pam is in a committed relationship, like ours*, I justified. *Amy and I get together all the time. Maybe they stopped for lunch. Maybe the health food store? Maybe coffee?*

It was nearing seven thirty. Dinner and I sat cold and waiting.

"Where have you been?"

"I lost track of time."

"You didn't answer your phone. Where have you been?"

She walked out of the room.

Time, the answer I thought could cure any problem, passed until Lori returned to the living room. "What is going on?" I demanded.

"Nothing, Emma, we just lost track of time."

Her eyes never met mine as I sat at one end of the camelback couch, in the room that had never felt big enough, waiting for her to become present. She picked up the remote control to the gas fireplace, recently installed, looking at the buttons as if she were figuring out which one to push to ignite the fire.

"I don't know how to tell you this," she spoke slowly, keeping her eyes on her tightened hand. "I think I've fallen in love with Pam."

Breathe, I silently instructed, somehow knowing these few words would be Lori's first and final acknowledgment. *Let her speak.* Our perpetual, unresolvable soap opera was reaching out for a climactic end. *Another betrayal.* I pushed away the thought. *Not another betrayal!*

Please, finish this relationship before you move into another, my mind begged her. She was already too deeply submerged in the seductive waters.

THIS TIME, NO DANCE CLASSES or costume designs would distract me from the pain. In therapy Lori held tight to the story that she was confused about what was happening. No chance of honest closure.

In the spare bedroom I lay in the dark, staring at the ceiling until the garage door hummed open, then shut as tightly as her heart had closed to me. Before she reached the first landing, I screamed through the row of poinsettias on the half wall. "I can't do this!" My voice reverberated in the deep stairwell. "I can't be living with you if you're committed to her."

The next morning I left for Kathleen and Jon's, where I canceled appointments daily until I could regain equilibrium. I returned home, centered myself in work, then fought, screamed, and resisted.

Finally, I insisted Lori move out and I began packing boxes of things that were *mine*, things that *she isn't gonna get*, stuff that *I might use when my life returns to... normal? What the hell is normal?* It didn't matter. Every box held a little more control. I piled them high in the rented storage unit and locked the door to keep them safe. Every day I wrapped more of myself and locked it away, only to return to my skeleton of a home with a *for sale* sign on the front lawn.

"You have to tell me why I've lost everything. Again!" I cried into the cellphone of the woman I was beginning to realize I no longer knew. "We have sold our home, my sanctuary, my beautiful garden. You said you'd never leave."

The truth, that we had grown apart, was something neither of us could say aloud. *What could I have done to deserve this?* My automatic "victim" tapes kicked on, fueled by the pulsing pain in my belly, bringing back to life my old familiar story. My tired frame curled into a tight sphere around the incessant longing to be loved as I pulled the blanket over my head and fell into an exhausted sleep on the living room floor of my newly rented apartment.

When I meditated, the stillness that slid in behind the agony was only temporary.

Intentional deep breathing released few of the feelings that arose without warning. My morning shower brought out the queasiness that threw me back to my knees, one hand gripping my head, the other my belly, as I folded in half until the emotions passed. Dripping wet, I made my way to the bedroom. *Why do I have to go through this?*

"I made a promise to stay conscious so this would never happen again," I lamented into the tapered candle. Julie had continually insisted that if I meditated and changed on the inside, circumstances would eventually, inevitably change on the outside. But Lori was supposed to change to fit into my life. She wasn't supposed to leave. "I supported her family. I did everything she asked. I'm constantly listening and witnessing," I cried into the bright flame. "She said she'd never leave me. How could she just walk out?" I slammed my fist on the floor. "Why is this happening to me again?"

Physical suffering? the voice asked. *Or letting go?*

I reeled forward, my hands pressed against my belly.

Your choice, it said.

"My choice?"

I FLOATED IN A HOT eucalyptus bath, feeling my anger, breathing deeply, and focusing on releasing its energy from every cell of my body. It felt toxic and old, dark and rancid. From some other world I eventually reached forward to pull the plug, and watched the water spiral down the drain.

Sitting naked, I stared into the slender flame and the open numerology book with passages underlined: *The number eleven designates an incarnation of testing.*

Yes, I'm being tested, but I can't free myself from the emotional pain of abandonment. This was the trigger that reconnected me to the stories of my father's betrayal, my husband's betrayal, my partner's betrayal.

In order to work at full capacity, I read from an oracle card, *you must be free to do what is necessary without restriction. Change is essential.* I closed my eyes to take it in.

No matter how much misery I was experiencing, I had to admit I was finally free. Now it was just me and God, me and The Divine Source, working together to face my most tormenting fear of not being loved. That fear had kept me running in repeated circles, reaching for the brass ring. I had drawn Lori to me as a soul mate so that I could come to this point and look at the question one more time. *Am I lovable? Am I loved? Do I truly believe I am?*

I closed my doors and didn't answer the phone, sat with the pain and repeated over and over, *I love you, Emma,* pushing away my impulses to return to Amy's front door in another heap of uncontrollable breakdown. Like the alcoholic stepping away from a drink, I turned from the gnawing pressure to dial Lori's number and spew another few choice words that could only temporarily release the pressure that weighed heavily on my heart. Alone in the darkness again, I breathed into the loveless ache and gently rocked it.

When I placed my pen to the paper, the words came forward without pause:

> *As painful as this is, it is necessary, Emma. It is your soul's will to move beyond it. This is why this moment has occurred. This is why we are in the feeling realms, because feelings must be observed, witnessed, honored, and lived through to the other side, where underlying beliefs are transformed.*
>
> *Stay with me here, Emma. True joy will not enter your heart until you overcome the obstacles of rebellious emotions and unruly thoughts. Joy is what you have come here to experience – true, deep joy that is always at your fingertips, waiting to be felt and embraced. Authentic, impenetrable joy! Unable to be broken down or dissolved. It is constantly available to you. Once you have touched upon this wellspring of joy, it is neverending. You are plugged into The Source. Unless you choose to unplug, it will always be your strength, your bliss, your true gift to others.*

CHAPTER 44

Thanksgiving

"Happy Birthday, Emma." All I can see are the orange and brown turkeys appliquéed on her oversized oven mitts as Kathleen's arms wrap around my shoulders. "The kids are planning something, so I'm supposed to tell you the upstairs is off limits to adults."

Light pours into her new kitchen, which doesn't hold a memory of the old Granville homestead. "We're setting up the buffet in the dining room," Kathleen adds with a wink, to let me know she's finally okay with freeing herself from the excessive formality of past Thanksgiving dinners. The table has been pushed to its smallest size and covered with a new tablecloth.

"Happy Birthday!" Gina's come in from the living room, just ahead of her husband. It was only a year before my relationship crumbled that hers was celebrated in the beautiful wedding ceremony she had always wished for. She raises her margarita and takes a sip before setting it down so we can share a good strong hug. "How's the apartment working out?"

"Good. I think this winter will be easier. New windows have been installed. When are you two heading to Florida?"

The sound of feet charging down the front stairs draws a gentle reprimand from Shari as she follows the line of children through Kathleen's new living room. "Mom," – she's nuzzling up to Kathleen, cupping a hand between her mouth and her mother's ear – "do you have some ribbons or old fabric we can use for head bands?"

Arms around each other, mother and daughter tap the little ones on their heads as they all disappear around the corner and patter back up the stairs. Peg has arrived. I can hear her chattering at the front door.

"You won't leave 'til after Christmas will you, Gina?" Jon is brushing his thinning silver hair over the bald spot that broadens with every visit. He holds a bottle of red wine retrieved from the cool basement. Jonathan is coming up the cellar stairs, laughing with two of his cousins.

"Aunt Emma!" the three of them shout in unison. Jonathan lifts a cold beer in a toast. "Did you just get here?" I nod my head. "The kids are busy..."

"I know. Something's brewing on the second floor."

We never celebrated the dramatic "final" Thanksgiving that we all had envisioned attending at the homestead. Our anticipation of the grand event passed as Jon and Kathleen retreated from their plan to sell and move for over a year. Their mid-summer call, announcing the news, was completely unexpected. Simply and quietly, the old Georgian homestead dropped out of our lives and was replaced by a contemporary colonial. We have all visited and gotten accustomed to this new home, with its large front porch and open floor plan. We have all let go and moved on.

I'm scanning the living room for signs of passing time, evident in the wrinkles that have formed around eyes that have lived nearly sixty years and a third generation that continues to spread their roots and grow tall. *We're doing okay*, I'm thinking. *More than okay.*

With all the strong traditions my sisters have embraced, I know I wasn't meant to mirror them. My journey was destined to be different. But every time I return home I'm grateful for the joy of it.

"What are you drinking, Emma?" Jon's waving an ice-filled glass over his head. "Gin and tonic?"

"That sounds great." I've turned to lean on the central island and tucked my foot around a leg of the bar stool, pulling it underneath me and taking a seat. "Something smells good." I look toward the faint smell of turkey, recently placed in the oven, making our proposed dinner time at least an hour later than planned.

"I peeled all the apples for two pies," Jon toasts to his own accomplishment with my cocktail.

"Okay, silence!" Josh calls from the living room. Little boys have fundamentally changed the dynamic of our family. Jonathan is setting up his ten-year-old's xylophone in front of Kathleen's piano, as Josh orchestrates the seating. "Aunt Peg, here" – he's pointing to the folding chair next to the fireplace – "and Nana" – one hand opens toward Kathleen as the other points insistently to her favorite upholstered chair.

Shari has plunked herself down on the floor with a child at each side, yin and yang. Marissa obediently rests her music on her lap as her brother Max squirms under his mother's guiding hand. The glances have already begun, from Peg to Gina, to me and back to Kathleen. Memory-filled emotions emerge as Josh folds back his music and places it before him.

"I'm going to play *Here Comes the Sun*," he announces, picking up his wooden mallets and returning to his audience for an aside. "I really like the Beatles." The ice tinkles in our glasses. Electronic drums have also been set up for him. "I composed this myself," he says, when he moves on to his second instrument. *Ah, the creative energy.*

As Marissa's long legs slide between the piano bench and keyboard the lump in my throat causes me to release an unanticipated sigh, not missed by Kathleen, who catches me dabbing away the tears. Exactly like her grandmother once did, the budding pianist fluffs her ruffled party dress and confidently places her foot on the pedal.

When she turns to receive her applause, Max rushes to take his sister's seat, running a tightened fist up and down all of the white keys, then standing to take the deepest bow. Our applause drops away into hugs and accolades, another moment of memory-making that will be stored away, deep in their hearts, with all the others. Down the road, along the way, those memories will be looked at again, as necessary in the forming of beliefs of how things are and why.

I wish for the children of our family a meaningful journey, rich with life experience, deep emotional connections, authentic power, and unbounded joy. We have no way of knowing what each of their processes will entail but we are all doing our best to help them feel the love that, I am hopeful, will lift them high as they fly wherever their souls are meant to go.

CHAPTER 45

The Affirmation

MY HEALING IS IN MY OWN HANDS

I'm on my way home, and beneath a huge tree under some leaves I uncover a large claw. I know it belonged to an eagle and was dropped just for me. When I pick it up I notice the softness at the base – but the tip is sharp.

Back in my room, I kneel on the floor, holding the claw that grows larger and larger. An extraordinary metamorphosis is taking place as the form of a large brown bird grows out of the claw and lies dead in my hands.

I feel a great love for this magnificent soul and, with a calm understanding, I begin to rock the dark form. When I place my hand on her cold closed wing, warmth radiates from my palms. Leaning forward, I set my ear over the eagle's heart and a faint beating seems to be growing stronger. I think I feel a breath but don't see how this could be possible.

As her breathing deepens, I consciously send energy to her heart and she begins to move, ever so slightly, rolling from my hands, miraculously righting herself on the floor before me. I can hardly believe the exquisite golden eagle is strong and standing upright. I'm sure she's too weak to fly.

She extends her wings to their fullest range and I can see they have been clipped. With a few confident downward strokes, she

Jan Johnson

lifts herself up and flies straight through the doorway, around the corner, and upward, along a far-reaching staircase.

My heart is open and ready to embark on the next phase of my journey, wherever the eagle takes me.

May it be so.

Acknowledgments

Karen Brown, Pat Summerer, and Sally Muir: my dear sisters who have supported this project from the beginning. Sally has helped me bring many of my dreams to life. Pat holds the vision of Oprah promoting my book. Karen has always believed in the power of dreams and freely offered them along the way, which has made shared dreaming an integral part of our sisterhood. Our love runs deep.

Peter J. Crowley: the photographer who returned to my life to bring my beautiful cover photographs forward. I have always admired the artist that you are, and I'm grateful for your remarkable gifts.

Louisa Calio: my soul sister, a poet and writer who opened my eyes to the metaphysical world. Your deep presence is aligned with heart and soul.

Nancy Moore Hulnick: a gifted artist and editor who offered to look at my manuscript when it was three hundred pages of rambling, then returned to bring it to its greatest potential. Thank you for your clear honest criticism, continued support, and deep friendship. I couldn't have done this without you.

Jacqueline Janes: an intuitive astrological therapist and friend for over thirty years. Because of your guidance I forged ahead in my life, and with the writing of this book. Your appreciation of the meaning in my first draft helped me hold the vision of a completed memoir. You remain a light on my path.

Robert Moss: the bestselling novelist, journalist, independent scholar and creator of *Active Dreaming*. Your playful, imaginative approach to understanding and expressing dreams has transformed the way I personally work with them. Because of journeys you have facilitated, I have, in your words: "made room for my bigger dreams to find me."

Jean Pieper: my spiritual partner and dreaming companion. Your commitment to being in authentic power is a constant invitation to be still and listen with an open heart. From this practice I have accessed a deeper understanding of myself.

Rita Riali: the *Persnickety Proofreader*. While making subtle changes and not altering my vision, you brought a sense of play to our initial editing. Your expertise and encouragement prepared me for the final revision. You were an integral step in meeting my goal.

All of my devoted friends who read many evolving manuscripts over the past ten years. I am grateful for your feedback and support on every level.

CPSIA information can be obtained at www.ICGtesting.com
Printed in the USA
BVOW062154240512

291049BV00001B/1/P